SKOKIE PUBLIC LIBRARY

3 1232 00671 6239

WITHDRAWN DEC 2012

Remember Your Manners

15 Reproducible Stories, 35 Teaching Posters, Activities, Role Play Ideas, and Guided Questions for Teaching Social Skills and Manners

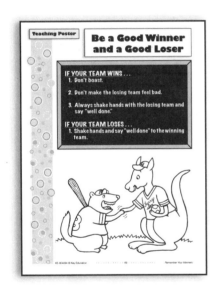

by
Jo Browning Wroe

Illustrated by
Julie Anderson

Key Education Publishing
An Imprint of Carson-Dellosa Publishing Company LLC
Greensboro, North Carolina

www.keyeducationpublishing.com

CONGRATULATIONS ON YOUR PURCHASE OF A KEY EDUCATION PRODUCT!

The editors at Key Education are former teachers who bring experience, enthusiasm, and quality to each and every product. Thousands of teachers have looked to the staff at Key Education for new and innovative resources to make their work more enjoyable and rewarding. We are committed to developing educational materials that will assist teachers in building a strong and developmentally appropriate curriculum for young children.

PLAN FOR GREAT TEACHING EXPERIENCES WHEN YOU USE EDUCATIONAL MATERIALS FROM KEY EDUCATION PUBLISHING COMPANY

Credits

Author: Jo Browning Wroe
Project Director: Sherrill B. Flora
Inside Illustrations: Julie Anderson
Editors: Claude Chalk & Karen Seberg
Page Design & Layout: Key Education Staff
Cover Design & Production: Annette Hollister-Papp

About the Author of the Stories

Jo Browning Wroe has taught both in the United Kingdom and in the United States. She earned her undergraduate degrees in English and Education from Cambridge University, Cambridge, England. She worked for 12 years in educational publishing before completing a Master's Degree in Creative Writing from the University of East Anglia, Norwich, England. Most of her time is now spent writing teacher resource materials and running workshops for others who love to write. Jo has been the recipient of the National Toy Libraries Award. She lives in Cambridge, England, with her two daughters, Alice and Ruby, and her husband, John.

Key Education

An imprint of Carson-Dellosa Publishing LLC
PO Box 35665
Greensboro, NC 27425 USA
www.keyeducationpublishing.com

Copyright Notice

© 2012, Carson-Dellosa Publishing LLC. The purchase of this material entitles the buyer to reproduce worksheets and activities for classroom use only—not for commercial resale. Reproduction of these materials for an entire school or district is prohibited. No part of this book may be reproduced (except as noted above), stored in a retrieval system, or transmitted in any form or by any means (mechanically, electronically, recording, etc.) without the prior written consent of Carson-Dellosa Publishing LLC. Key Education is an imprint of Carson-Dellosa Publishing LLC.

Printed in the USA • All rights reserved.

ISBN 978-1-602681-114-9

Contents

Introduction

For children to be successful in LIFE, they need to be TAUGHT social skills, manners, and etiquette, as well as academic skills. If we truly want all children to succeed, educators must stress the importance of polite and acceptable behavior—and teach the social skills needed for making and keeping friends, becoming an honest and responsible citizen, and eventually using these skills as adults to find and maintain employment.

Social skills and manners should be taught to all children, but it is especially important that teaching these skills become part of curriculum for children with Autism Spectrum Disorders. Teaching these skills will help children with autism develop a better understanding common social situations as well as helping them learn manners and appropriate social responses.

Remember Your Manners uses a teacher's guide, stories with large pictures, teaching posters, activities, guided questions, and role-playing to teach manners and social skills. Each engaging story relates to a specific manner or social situation. The visual approach along with the guided questions and role-playing practice is ideal for all children, but is especially effective for children with autism.

Unit 1
Those Magic Words

Story Summary

When an enticing candy store opens in the neighborhood, Ollie's mother agrees to give him money to spend there on an end-of-the-week treat. When Friday comes, a hungry Ollie runs ahead of his mother and charges into the store. In his desperation to buy the candy, he is impolite and offends the woman who owns the shop. After each rude interchange, certain physical changes come over the owner. By the time his mom arrives, Ollie has been ordered to leave the store. At home, his mom explains that if Ollie doesn't speak politely to people, they will react negatively to him. However, if he uses the magic words, people will respond well. After practicing at home, Ollie returns to the store, apologizes, and uses all of the magic words he knows. The store's owner is pleased with his good manners and even gives Ollie some free candy.

Concepts

The story makes the point that polite words (listed below) can work magic on people. In contrast, if people are treated rudely, they will often become angry and respond negatively. The story also reminds children not to forget their magic words, even when they are in a rush, are disappointed, or want something very badly.

Please   Thank you   No, thank you   You're welcome   May I?   Excuse me   I'm sorry

Read the Story: "The Candy Store"

Reproduce the story found on pages 7–12. Staple the pages together in numerical order and read them to the class.

Guided Questions

1. When Ollie enters the candy store, he points at the candy that looks like strawberries and says, "How much are those?" What should Ollie say instead when he first goes into the store?

2. When Ollie finds out the strawberry candy is made of marzipan (which he dislikes), what could he say that would be more polite?

3. What else does Ollie say to the woman or what does he do that makes her angry?

4. Why does Ollie forget to be polite when he is in the store?

5. When might you forget to be polite? (*in a hurry, upset, in a bad mood, shy, too excited*)

6. Why does Ollie's mom call polite words "magic" words?

7. When Ollie is rude to the woman who owns the store, how does she change?

8. In real life, people don't grow horns, and their eyes don't turn red, but what might happen if you are rude to a grown-up? How might the grown-up react?

Role-Play Ideas

1. There is a long line for the bathroom in a restaurant. The child at the end of the line is desperate and knows she can't wait. She must ask the other people in the line if she can go to the front. At first, she is rude, but then she remembers her magic words.

2. Role-play a scene at the movies. People in the front row talk after the movie starts and noisily unwrap candy. Their behavior is spoiling the movie for the people behind them, who then ask them to be quiet. Enact the conversation without using polite words; repeat using polite words. Which was more effective?

3. A teacher scolds a student, but it is for something he didn't do. The student is angry and upset. He must explain that he is not at fault. How can he be respectful to the teacher while still getting his point across?

Those Magic Words

Please

excuse me

Thank you

I'm sorry

you're welcome

may I?

no, thank you

**Saying magic words makes people happy.
Not saying magic words
makes people unhappy.
It's that simple!**

The Candy Store

Ollie was thrilled when a little candy store opened on the corner of his street.

"Can we go in?" he asked his mom on the Monday after it opened.

"On Friday," she said, "for an end-of-the-week treat."

On Tuesday, Wednesday, and Thursday, Ollie looked in the window and dreamed about the candy he would buy with the two dollars his mom has promised him. Toffee? Chocolate? Fudge? Or, chocolate-covered fudge? What about the candy that looked like strawberries? What were they made of? He liked strawberries—as long as they weren't marzipan. He didn't like that. How many could he buy for two dollars? There were no prices, only trays and trays of delicious candy.

Friday afternoon arrived at last. Ollie ran along the sidewalk. "Come on, Mom," he shouted, but she was a long way behind. So, he burst into the store on his own.

Ollie had been excited about buying candy all week, but he still didn't know what he was going to get.

"How much are those?" He pointed at the strawberries. "What are they made of?"

"Good afternoon to you too!" said the tiny woman, who looked about a hundred. "They're marzipan and 20 cents each." The woman had short gray hair and sharp blue eyes.

"I hate marzipan," Ollie said, disappointed. "What about these?" As he pointed at the toffees, he accidentally knocked two pieces off the tray.

"Careful!" The woman glared at Ollie. He jumped. Her blue eyes had turned red!

"I want some fudge," Ollie said, holding out his dollars. He wanted to get his candy and run.

The woman knelt down to pick up the toffee pieces. Ollie jumped again. Two little horns were poking through her hair!

"Get a move on!" Ollie said, scared and hungry at the same time.

The woman stood up and put her face close to Ollie's.

"You are the rudest child I've ever met! Get out of my store!"

"You're mean—and, and, you're ugly!" Ollie shouted in a panic. That's when Ollie's mom walked in, just in time to hear her son being so rude.

As soon as they got home, Ollie ran upstairs and slammed his bedroom door.

"Ollie, come down," called his mom. "We need to talk!"

"No!" he yelled. "That woman's weird!"

A few minutes later, there was a tap at his bedroom door. It was his mom with a glass of milk and a cookie.

"Did you see her?" asked Ollie. "She shouldn't come out till Halloween."

"What I saw was you being very rude," said Mom. "She is a nice old woman who expects children to have manners. I know you're not really rude, but people will get upset if you forget to be polite."

"I didn't mean to upset her."

"It's the way the world works, Ollie. Those polite words—they're like magic. If you use them, people are happy; if you don't, they're not. It's as simple as that."

"Remind me what the magic words are," said Ollie.

His mom smiled. "I'll give you a quick lesson. Then, we're going back to that store, and you're going to use your magic."

"I'm scared. She had horns and red eyes."

"Nonsense. She's a sweet little old lady. You'll see."

Half an hour later, a nervous Ollie stepped back into the store. He was relieved to see the woman's eyes were blue again, and the only thing on her head was hair.

"Hello," he said. His mom nudged him. "I'm sorry I was rude. I was so excited about the candy, I forgot my magic words." The woman smiled, even though it looked as if she was trying not to. "Please," Ollie said, "could you tell me how much your fudge is?"

"Certainly. It's 50 cents each."

"Thank you," Ollie said. He wanted to look at the candy behind the woman, but she was in the way. "Excuse me, but may I look over here?"

"You may," said the woman, stepping aside. Her eyes seemed to twinkle. "Would you like some of those?" she asked after a moment.

"No, thank you," Ollie said. "But, I'd like four pieces of fudge, please." As the woman started to put them in a bag, he said, "I love your store."

"Well, thank you," she smiled, twisting the top of the bag closed.

"You're welcome," Ollie said.

Then, he whispered to his mom, "Have I forgotten any words?"

"I think you've got it covered," she whispered back.

"Do you think they worked?"

"I think so. Look."

The woman was reaching for a chocolate. "And, here's an extra piece for you—these are my favorite."

"But, I've used all my money," Ollie said.

"This one's on me. You were brave to come back, and I do love good manners." The woman handed him the chocolate. "See you next week?"

"You bet!" said Ollie. "Thank you."

"You're welcome!" said the sweet little old lady.

The End

Story Summary

Barney is a rabbit from a very large family. Living with nine older sisters and eight older brothers, Barney has learned that he must fight to get attention by being loud, tough, and bossy. When he starts school and is in a class larger than his family, he thinks he will have to be even louder, tougher, and bossier. Barney quickly finds out that this is not the way to make friends outside of his burrow. After a disastrous first day, Barney learns to adjust his behavior, and he makes some new friends.

Concepts

This story and the following questions and role-play ideas encourage children to think about their behavior towards others, such as getting along; not boasting, being bossy, or tattling; sharing; taking turns; cooperating; being kind; involving others; and being a good sport.

Children should also be encouraged to learn how to join a group:

1. Watch a group of kids playing and observe what is happening.

2. Show interest in the group.

3. Ask to join in.

4. Be prepared to handle rejection with grace in case those in the group do not want you to join them.

Read the Story: "Rabbits Can Make Friends Too!"

Reproduce the story found on pages 17–24. Staple the pages together in numerical order and read them to the class.

Guided Questions

1. Why is Barney so rude, bossy, and loud?

2. Why does Barney think he will have to be even more rude and loud when he goes to school?

3. What is the first mistake Barney makes when he goes into the classroom?

4. What would be a better way for Barney to choose where he will sit?

5. When the teacher tells him he has to wait his turn and ask politely for things, what does Barney think will happen if he does this?

6. When Barney tries to play with the other animals, what does he do wrong?

7. What would be a better way to go about joining in a game?

8. Why do you think Barney doesn't want the squirrels to come to play at his house?

Role-Play Ideas

1. A group of friends is playing during recess. There is a new boy in the class. He is standing off by himself. Role-play how the group can be friendly to him even though at first he doesn't say much.

2. Role-play a scene where some friends are playing a new game. One person loses and is a bad sport; she becomes angry and stomps off. Next, act out a scene where the person is still not the winner of the game, but she handles her disappointment well.

3. Talk through the steps (see the Concepts section above and the Teaching Poster on page 16) for joining a group. Then, ask children to act out the part of someone who wants to join others in a game. Do a version of the scene where the child follows the steps and is successful and another version where the child is not invited to join the game.

How to Be a Good Friend

Good friends take turns and share.

Good friends are kind.

Good Friends Do Not . . .

Good friends **DO NOT** boast or brag.

They **DO NOT** bully others.

They **ARE NOT** bossy.

How to Make New Friends

1. **Watch groups of kids playing. Observe what is happening.**

2. **Show interest in the group.**

3. **Ask to join in.**

4. **Be prepared to handle rejection. Sometimes, the answer might be no.**

   Be nice because next time the kids might say yes.

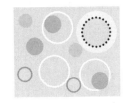

Rabbits Can Make Friends Too!

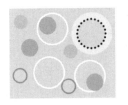

Barney came from a big family. He had nine older sisters and eight older brothers. Barney was a rabbit.

Barney's parents loved him. His brothers and sisters loved him. But, his parents were always busy, fixing the burrow, mending clothes, cooking, and tidying up. His brothers and sisters were always busy playing, arguing, and going to school.

Barney had learned that to be noticed, he had to shout the loudest, cry the hardest, or be the naughtiest. By the time Barney was old enough for school, he was tougher, ruder, and louder than his tough, rude, and loud brothers and sisters. What no one had time to tell him was that this was not how it worked outside the family's busy burrow.

Barney knew there would be more animals in his class than brothers and sisters at home. He thought he would need to turn up his volume, stand his ground, and watch out for himself even more at school.

Poor Barney.

On his first day of school, Barney hopped into the classroom. He saw a seat that he wanted at the front of the class. A badger had already hung her bag over the back of it and was just brushing off her tail. Barney had to be quick! He leaped over the desk and landed in the seat, knocking the badger's bag off and onto the floor. Then, he smiled at the badger. He always smiled when he got his way.

The angry badger went straight to the teacher. The teacher frowned.
"Barney! What do you think you are doing? Say you are sorry to Sally."
"Sorry." Barney was still smiling, still in the seat.
"And?" said the teacher.
"And, what?" said Barney.
"And, give Sally her seat back!"
"It's mine!"
"That's not how we behave in this classroom, young rabbit. You come and sit next to me."
The teacher glared at him. Sally glared at him. The whole class glared at him.

At recess time, his teacher asked him to stay behind. "Barney, you mustn't do that again. You can't just barge in and take something that's not yours."

"Then, how on earth will I get what I want?"

"Wait your turn. Or, ask nicely."

Barney laughed. "Wait my turn? Ask nicely? That will never work."

Barney's teacher looked at him. "Barney, you'll find you won't have many friends here if you carry on like that."

Barney went out to the playground. His classmates were all playing a game of tag. When they saw him, they stopped and turned their backs. Barney leaped over to them.

"I'll be it!" He thumped his strong back leg on the ground.

"Are you nuts?" said a chipmunk. "We don't even like you."

"I'm it," Barney tried again. "I'll punch you if I can't be it."

Slowly, the animals walked away. "They really don't like me," Barney thought, puzzled. Even when his brothers and sisters got annoyed with him at home, he always knew they loved him.

By the end of his first day at school, Barney had gotten into three arguments and two fights and made three ferrets cry.

Walking to school the next day, Barney had a feeling he hadn't had in a long time. He wanted to cry. At school, his teacher said they should each find a partner and then build models of their homes using Legos. Barney thought no one would want to work with him, so he started to build a Lego burrow all by himself.

"Do you want some help?" It was Sally, the badger.

"Oh! Um, OK," he said. No one had ever offered him help before.

"I'm not very good at building," he admitted.

Sally smiled, "I'll help you. I am a very good builder."

Together, they built a fantastic burrow. Sally couldn't believe what a big house Barney lived in.

When it was time for recess, they went outside together.

"The others won't want me to play with them," said Barney.

"If you ask nicely, they might let you play. They only said no yesterday because you were bossy," explained Sally.

Barney said, "I have to be like that at home to be noticed."

"Go and ask the squirrels if you can join them. They like to run around at recess," Sally suggested.

Barney was nervous, but he hopped over to the squirrels. "Hi. Sally said you like to run around. Can we run around together?"

"As long as you don't hit us." The squirrels looked scared.

Barney said, "I won't hit you! I just want to run around a bit."

Barney saw Sally from across the playground. She smiled and gave him a thumbs up.

"Nice tails by the way," Barney said to the squirrels.

The squirrels looked pleased. "Thanks. Nice ears."

"Thanks," said Barney. He'd never had a compliment before. It made him feel good.

They ran around the playground a few times and then stood panting.

"That was great," said one of the squirrels. "Would you like to play at my house after school? Or, could we come to your house?"

"I think it might be better to play at your house, if you don't mind," said Barney.

The End

Unit 3
Good Hygiene

Story Summary

It is the first day of preschool at Washington Zoo. Miss Mirkett, a meerkat, tells the young animals that, regardless of what their families do at home, they must observe certain hygiene rules at school, both before they come and when they are there—even if some rules go against the grain! Miss Mirkett talks through seven rules of hygiene, acknowledging the problems that following them might entail for certain class members.

Concepts

This story and the following questions and role-play ideas encourage children to follow basic rules of hygiene, such as brush your teeth and wash your hair; don't pick your nose in public; cover your mouth when coughing or sneezing; don't make bodily noises; and wash your hands often, especially before meals, after using the bathroom, and whenever they are dirty.

Read the Story: "Miss Mirkett's Strange Rules"

Reproduce the story found on pages 29–36. Staple the pages together in numerical order and read them to the class.

Guided Questions

1. What kinds of animals are in Miss Mirkett's class?

2. Before she starts to describe the new hygiene rules, Miss Mirkett tells the students a few other things they mustn't do. What are they?

3. What does Charlie, the chimp, and his family do together every night after tea?

4. What does Miss Mirkett say they must not do with the soap?

5. Why does Miss Mirkett insist that Alasdair brush his teeth before school?

6. What happens to hair if it is not washed (apart from it looking bad)?

7. What animal in last year's class had to leave the room to sneeze? Why?

8. What does Miss Mirkett tell the students they are going to learn after recess?

Role-Play Ideas

1. Act out a scene in Miss Mirkett's class where she teaches her students how to handle a toothbrush. Have her use Alasdair as an example during the lesson and find all kinds of interesting things in his teeth.

2. Role-play Lolli's mom coming to school to complain about having to wash Lolli's hair. What might Miss Mirkett say to Lolli's mom? Encourage students to make the conversation funny.

3. Miss Mirkett is invited to have tea one afternoon with Charlie's family. Have students enact the scene at the chimpanzees' house.

Good Hygiene = Good Manners

Rule Number 1.
Keep your body clean.
Take baths using soap and warm water.

Rule Number 2.
Brush your teeth at least twice day.

Rule Number 3.
Wash your hair several times a week.

Good Hygiene = Good Manners

Rule Number 4.
Always cover your mouth when you sneeze or cough. And then, go and wash your hands!

Rule Number 5.
Always wash your hands before you eat and after visits to the bathroom. Washing hands frequently gets rid of bad germs.

Good Hygiene = Good Manners

Rule Number 6.

No nose picking.
Nose picking, if it must be done, is done alone and remember to use a tissue.

Rule Number 7.

All of us sometimes make certain bodily noises. Sometimes it just happens. Then, we should say, "Excuse me." What we don't do is make the noises on purpose.

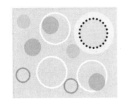
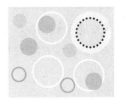

Miss Mirkett's Strange Rules

Good morning, students. My name is Miss Mirkett. Welcome to Washington Zoo School. You're here to learn to read, write, and count. You're all clever young animals. But first, we have a few other things that you might find a little harder to learn. Here at the zoo, we have such a variety of animals! Look around and see what a mixed bunch you are.

We have a chimpanzee. Hello, Charlie. We have a two-toed sloth. Hello, Lolli. We have a hippo. Hello, Henry. And, we have a darling little alligator. Hello, Alasdair. I'm your teacher and, as you can see, I'm a meerkat.

What you must understand is that normal family rules do not apply here at school. We have our own rules. They may seem strange, but I insist upon them. And, I hope it goes without saying, there is to be no fighting, no biting, and absolutely no chasing or eating your classmates. Understood? Wonderful!

Now, on to the new rules.

Number 1. Don't even come to class if you haven't said hello to a bar of soap and warm water. I do understand you like the smell of your bodies, and you like the smell of your parents' bodies. Some of you even spray your smells around to feel at home. Well, not here, no sirree! Your body might smell good to you and your loved ones, but it certainly doesn't smell good to the rest of us.

This thing I have in my hand now is a bar of soap. Soap is often white, but it does come in other colors. Do not eat soap. Trust me, you won't like it. Last year, a little goat was foaming from the mouth for days.

Number 2. Brush your teeth. Now, Alasdair, for an alligator this is a big job. You may need some help. The thing is, honey, if you've eaten a bucketful of fish for breakfast, no matter how much I like you, when you read at my desk and breathe all over me, I won't be happy. No one wants to smell what you ate for breakfast. I have toothbrushes in my drawer. We'll learn how to use them later.

Number 3. Next is hair washing. Lolli, this is a big task for you. When you're at home with mommy and daddy, hanging upside down with mold growing in your hair and little nits running around, I guess that's fine. But, in my class—I'm sorry, sweetheart—it's just plain nasty. Dirty hair looks bad and it smells. At Washington Zoo School, we insist on clean hair. So tomorrow, everyone should come to school with clean hair!

Number 4. It's nearly winter, so you will get coughs and colds. But, if some of you let rip with a huge sneeze, you could, quite frankly, blow me away. Think of all the germs that come flying out of your mouths and snouts at over a hundred miles an hour. It's a wonder I survive each winter! Once, I had a young elephant in my class who had to go outside when he felt a sneeze coming on. So, always, always, always cover your mouths when you sneeze or cough. And then, go and wash your hands, claws, and paws!

Number 5. I mentioned washing hands, claws, and paws after sneezing or coughing, but we also need to wash our hands, claws, and paws before lunch. And, washing is very important after a visit to the bathroom. You all bring special gifts to class, but, sorry to say, you all bring special germs, too. And, that's one thing we don't want to share. Before we eat and after a visit to the bathroom, we all must wash our hands.

Number 6. I must have no nose or snout picking. I knew you'd look surprised, Charlie. Last year, your sister explained that's what your family does together after tea each night. "Not here, little chimp," I had to say. Nose picking, if done at all, is done alone. I have tissues, but I'd rather you leave your noses and snouts alone in class.

And finally, **Rule Number 7**.

I never know quite how to put this. All of us, from time to time, need to . . . shall we say . . . make certain . . . noises, sometimes from our mouths and sometimes from somewhere else—that little place, hidden for most of you, under your tails. Yes, I know you don't have a tail, Charlie. Never mind. Some of you may call this burping or belching and passing gas. No giggling, this really is not funny!

Of course, all of us can get taken by surprise sometimes and it just happens. So, then we say, "Excuse me," and get on with what we're doing. What we don't do is make the noises deliberately, make them be as loud as possible, or smell each other's smells. OK, you can all stop giggling right now.

After recess, we're going to learn how to make soap go frothy and how much toothpaste to put on your toothbrush. If all goes well, we might even have time for a story.

The End

Unit 4
Mealtime Manners

Story Summary

William is being raised by two elderly grandparents. He is quite old-fashioned and doesn't play like the other children his age, but he is very polite and well mannered. At William's school, each class sits together to eat lunch. Miss Hall, the teacher, sees an opportunity during the meal to get William more involved with his classmates and to build up his confidence. She films the students eating their lunches and then asks William to point out where their manners are lacking. William rises to the occasion and his friends are surprised at how much they don't know.

Concepts

Children are encouraged to wait for everyone to sit before eating, use napkins, eat with utensils instead of their hands, sit up straight and not put their elbows on the table, keep their mouths closed and not overfill them, not burp or slurp, be willing to try new foods, ask politely if they want something instead of grabbing or stretching over people, and not leave the table until everyone's finished,

Read the Story: "Mealtime Movie"

Reproduce the story found on pages 41–48. Staple the pages together in numerical order and read them to the class.

Guided Questions

1. Why do you think William has such very good manners?

2. What does Miss Hall notice about William when the class is eating lunch together?

3. What is the first thing that William sees the class doing wrong?

4. In what other ways do William's friends forget to use good mealtime manners?

5. Which manners are to make everyone feel equally important? (*don't start eating until everyone's seated, ask politely if something is wanted instead of grabbing, don't leave the table until everyone's finished*) Which manners are to stop gross things from happening? (*use a napkin, chew with your mouth closed*)

6. Why do you think you shouldn't put your elbows on the table?

7. How does William feel after this lesson?

8. Is there one table manner that you think is the most important? Why?

Role-Play Ideas

1. Role-play a scene where William takes his friends Paul and Toby home to share a meal with his strict grandparents.

2. Act out a mealtime where no one has any manners at all!

3. Act out a mealtime where everyone has perfect manners.

Table Manners— Getting Ready to Eat

Reminder 1:
It is polite to wait to begin eating until everyone is seated.

Reminder 2:
Always use a napkin. It will protect your clothes, and it can be used to wipe off your hands or mouth.

Reminder 3:
Remember to keep your elbows off the table.

Reminder 4:
Sit up straight and no slouching while eating a meal.

Table Manners— Eating the Meal

Reminder 5:
DO NOT eat with your fingers! Use silverware!

Reminder 6:
DO NOT chew with your mouth open!

Reminder 7:
DO NOT talk with food in your mouth!

Reminder 8:
DO NOT burp or belch!

Reminder 9:
DO NOT put too much food in your mouth!

Reminder 10:
DO NOT slurp with straws or when sipping soup!

Teaching Poster

Table Manners—
Eating & Ending
the Meal

Reminder 11:
If you want something from across the table, ask politely for it to be passed to you. Do not grab things.

Reminder 12:
If someone has cooked a new food for you, it's polite to try it. How will you know if you like it, if you don't try it?

Salad Dressing

Reminder 13:
Wait to leave the table until everyone has finished eating. You may ask to be excused in an emergency, such as needing to use the bathroom.

Reminder 14:
When you are finished eating, clear your dishes and then push in your chair.

Mealtime Movie

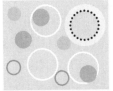
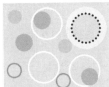

William lived with his very rich, very old grandparents. William had no brothers or sisters. He could already read and write when he started school. He knew his times tables and could name all of the states in the United States of America and all of the capital cities of Europe.

When his grandmother took him to school on the first day, William wore a necktie, a white shirt, a navy blue jacket, and polished leather shoes. Grandmother saw that the other children were wearing blue jeans, tennis shoes, and T-shirts.

Back home after dropping William off at school, Grandmother said to William's grandfather, "Things have changed more than I realized since we went to school."

"Hardly surprising, my dear," he said, "since that was 75 years ago."

"Goodness me, so it was. I hope William will get along all right.'"

The other children liked strange little William. He was quiet, but he was a kind boy who smiled and said please and thank you a lot.

"Want to play with me?" Toby asked on William's first day.

"What do you mean?" said William.

"What do you mean, what do you mean?" said a surprised Toby. "Play what?"

"Whatever we want."

Toby showed William how to run around and play, but William was not used to it. Often, he preferred to sit quietly and think or read.

Miss Hall kept a close eye on William. She wanted to make sure he felt like he was part of the class.

Summerfield Elementary School had a nice lunchroom. Every day, each class sat together and ate lunch as a group. Miss Hall knew her students were noisy and chaotic at lunchtime. Then, she noticed William. He was sitting at the end of a table with a napkin tucked into his shirt, eating his meal quietly. Miss Hall had a brilliant idea.

The next day at lunch, the children were surprised to see Miss Hall filming them while they ate. Miss Hall explained that after lunch they would all understand why she was making a "mealtime movie."

Back in the classroom, Miss Hall asked William to come to the front of the class. She handed him a brass bell.

"William," she said, "we're going to watch the film of our meal. Ring this bell every time you see bad manners at the table."

The class laughed to see themselves on-screen, but it was only seconds before William rang the bell. Ding.

"I hadn't even sat down," said William, "and some of them have started to eat. You shouldn't start until everyone is sitting down."

"Quite right, William. Got that everyone?"

Ding. William rang the bell again. "No one is using a napkin!"

"A what?" said Paul, who sat next to William.

"Tell the class why a napkin is useful, William," said Miss Hall.

"It protects your clothes, and you can wipe your hands or mouth on it."

Ding again.

William said, "Paul's picking up food with his fingers! That's what his silverware is for."

Ding. "Paul's eating with his mouth open. Do we really want to see chewed-up potato? I don't think so." William was getting into this. Miss Hall was smiling. Ding.

"Now, he's talking with his mouth full. Look! Did a piece of meat fly out onto Emily's plate?"

"Gross, Paul!" said Emily. "Don't do that!"

"Can't you pick on somebody else?" said Paul. "I'm not the only gross one."

"Sorry," said William. "I'll stop picking on you, but—oh, Paul!" Ding. "You burped! You really shouldn't do that!"

Everyone laughed, and even Paul couldn't help smiling.

Ding. William rang the bell again.

"Emily's elbows are on the table."

"Sorry," said Emily, going red and sliding her elbows off her desk.

"It's OK to do it in class, Emily," said Miss Hall, "just not at meals."
Emily put her elbows back on her desk.

"And really, Emily, you should sit up straight," carried on William. He was enjoying himself, "A lazy back shows a lazy mind."

"Sorry," said Emily, sitting up straight.

Ding.

"Sarah has too much food in her mouth. She can't even close it."

"Yeah," said Paul, glad William wasn't talking about him. "Your mouth's not a garbage can."

"Hush, Paul. Let's listen to William and not you," said Miss Hall.

Ding. "Did you ear that noise?" exclaimed William. "I can't see who did it, but someone made a terrible slurping sound. I think the sound might have been with a straw."

"Whoops, that was me drinking from my juice box," said Toby. "It's not fair, Miss Hall. You didn't get me on camera."

"I think you're coming up next, Toby. There you are!"

Ding. "He's just reached across Caroline to get the ketchup. Look! His sleeve has gone in her gravy."

"Yuck, Toby," said Caroline.

"Sorry. Why did you have to film me right then, Miss Hall?"

"If you want something from across the table," William said, "ask politely. Don't grab things."

Ding. "Carla's making a face at the broccoli."

"I'd never had it before!" said Carla. "It smelled horrible."

"If someone's cooked it for you, it's polite to try it. How will you know if you like it, if you don't try it?"

Ding.

"Look," said William. "Toby left the table before everyone was finished eating!"

"But, I needed to go to the bathroom," said Toby.

"You should wait to leave the table until everyone has finished. You shouldn't get up, except in an emergency. Then, you ask to be excused."

The movie was over. The class clapped, and William had a wide grin.

"Did you enjoy that, William?" asked Miss Hall.

"Yes," said William. "I just repeated all the things that my grandmother says to me every night at the dinner table. I should invite everyone to my house for dinner! Grandmother would see that I really have learned my mealtime manners!"

The End

Unit 5
Phone Manners

Story Summary

At the movies with her dad, Grace is angry and embarrassed when his cell phone rings, and he holds a conversation while people are trying to watch the movie. Back at home, Grace is busy telling her mother how awful the experience was when their landline phone rings. Someone asks if her father is there. Still upset, Grace simply says no and hangs up. Later, she finds out the call was from the movie theater with the message that her father's cell phone had been found there. Because she failed to take the message properly and politely, her father was greatly inconvenienced. Grace's mother teasingly admonishes her family for their bad phone manners but then makes her own phone manners mistake.

Concepts

Making a call
- Do not make a phone call too early in the morning or too late at night.
- Always say your name and the person you are calling. "Hello, this is _____. May I speak to _____?"

Answering
- Answer with a clear hello and speak clearly.
- When responding say, "Just a moment, please" or "Please wait, I'll get _____" or "_____ cannot come to the phone right now. May I please take a message?"
- Always end a call by saying thank you and good-bye. Never just hang up.

Cell phone
- Do not use a cell phone in the car; in a church, a temple, a mosque, a movie theater, or a library; at a table in a restaurant; or at a sporting event. Be polite and considerate of others around you—do not talk too loudly!

Read the Story: "A Bad Day for Phones"

Reproduce the story found on pages 53–58. Staple the pages together in numerical order and read them to the class.

Guided Questions

1. What are the two mistakes that Grace's dad makes at the movies with his cell phone? (*doesn't turn it off, answers it when it rings and holds a conversation*)

2. What is wrong with the way Grace answers the phone when she is home after the movie?

3. What happens as a result of Grace not answering the phone properly?

4. Grace's dad promises not to use his phone at the movies. Where else should we not use cell phones?

5. What does Grace promise to do whenever she answers the phone?

6. How do we know that Grace's mom thinks she has better phone manners than Grace or Grace's dad?

7. What mistake does Grace's mom make when using the phone?

8. What time do you think is too early to call people on the phone? Too late?

Role-Play Ideas

1. Have pairs of children role-play good phone manners. One child can make the call and the other answers using the suggestions in the Concepts section above. Then, have them switch roles.

2. Role-play scenes in various settings, such as in a library or at a concert, where one person has forgotten to turn off her phone. What happens after it rings? Enact different outcomes depending on whether the person chooses to use good phone manners or not.

Teaching Poster

Phone Manners— Answering the Phone

If the person IS NOT home . . .

Phone Manners— Using a Cell Phone

Cell Phone Manners to Remember

- Do not talk on the phone with (or text) someone else when you are talking face-to-face with people.

- Do not talk about personal things if people are near who may overhear your conversation.

- Talk quietly so that you do not disturb others.

- Try to stay at least 10 feet away from others while talking on a cell phone.

- Remember to be considerate!

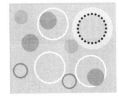
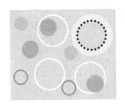

A Bad Day for Phones

"I'm never going to the movies with Dad again!" Grace had come into the kitchen and thrown her bag on the floor. "I was so embarrassed. He ruined it for everyone!"

"Slow down!" said Grace's mom. "What happened?"

"He didn't turn his cell phone off and it rang—twice!"

"Oh dear," said Grace's mom.

"It rang during the really quiet parts of the movie."

"Oh no," said Grace's mom.

"And—he answered it!"

"How could he?" Grace's mom was a bit angry now too.

"People were pointing at us and frowning, but he didn't notice because he was on the phone."

"Sounds like your dad needs a lesson in cell phone manners. He should know you don't use them at the movies or anywhere like that. Where is he anyway?"

"He's back at work. He said he'll be home late."

Just then, the house phone rang. Grace was still cross. She snatched the phone. "What?" she said.

Her mom's eyebrows shot up in surprise.

"He's not here." Grace said and put the phone down.

"Who was that?" said Grace's mom.

"I don't know."

"Grace, that was so rude!"

"No, it wasn't." Grace just wanted to complain more about her dad.

"You're as bad as your father! You need to remember your phone manners too!"

"What did I do wrong?"

"You didn't answer politely and say hello, you didn't ask who was calling, and you didn't offer to take a message or ask the person to call back. In fact, all you said to the poor person was, 'What?'"

"What else was there to say?"

"How about, 'Can I take a message? Would you like him to call you back?' How about, 'Thanks, good-bye'? You hung up without saying anything. Really, Grace, that was very rude."

"Sorry," said Grace.

That night, Grace was watching TV with her mom. When her dad came in, she had forgotten how angry she'd been with him. Now, he was the one who looked mad.

"What's wrong?" asked Grace's mom.

"After I dropped Grace back home from the movies, I had a meeting in town. When I got there, I couldn't find my cell phone. I went everywhere I'd been that afternoon. Finally, I went to the movie theater. They had it!"

"That's good," said Grace. "So, why are you mad?"

"Because," Grace's dad said with his hands on his hips, "they said they'd called my home number, but a rude young woman answered and then hung up before they could explain they had my phone."

"Whoops!" Grace said. "Sorry, Dad."

"Why were you so rude?" he asked.

"Because," said Grace, "I was still mad at you for talking during the movie."

"I'm sorry about that," Grace's dad said, now looking more embarrassed than angry. "I won't use my cell phone at the movies again."

"Or, at church or in a restaurant," said Grace's mom.

"OK, OK," said Grace's dad holding up his hands. "I promise."

"Good," said Grace, "or I'm not going out with you ever again."

"Just a minute," said Grace's mom. "You need to remember a few things too, don't you?"

"Yes," Grace said. "I must answer politely, say hello and ask if I can take a message, or ask the caller to wait while I get the person they want."

"Oh!" said Grace's mom. "All this talk about phone calls reminds me. I need to call Sarah. We've got a bake sale this week." She picked up the phone and winked at them both. "Watch and learn, rude phone people. See how it's meant to be done."

She dialed the number. "Hello, this is Carla Walker. May I please speak to Sarah?" She put her hand over the receiver and whispered, "Did you notice how I said hello and my name and then I asked for the person I wanted? I don't know why you two find it so hard to use your phone manners."

Suddenly, Grace's mom was listening carefully; someone on the phone was talking to her.

"Sarah, I'm so sorry," she said, her face turning red. "I didn't realize how late it was! Of course, I'll call you back tomorrow." She put the phone down. "How embarrassing! It's after 10 o'clock. She was fast asleep!"

"So, another rule when we're using the phone . . ." said Grace's dad smiling.

"I know, I know," said Grace's mom. "Don't call people too late."

"Or, too early!" said Grace. "I wouldn't remember my phone manners if someone woke me up early on a Saturday morning."

"Speaking of sleep," said Grace's mom, "it's time for bed."

"I'm glad you got your phone back, Dad," said Grace, "and glad you promised not to be a cell phone monster any more."

Her dad laughed, picked up a cushion, and tossed it at Grace. She ducked, and the cushion hit the phone on wall behind her. The receiver fell off and bumped against the countertop.

"It really hasn't been a good day for phones in this house, has it?" said Grace.

The End

Unit 6
Meet & Greet Manners

Story Summary

Mr. Smith's class is full of very friendly, enthusiastic children. He likes them a lot but knows that they often forget their manners when they become excited. The principal, Mrs. Wood, warns Mr. Smith that a very important visitor is coming to their class, and he has to make sure his students know how to meet and greet the visitor correctly. Mr. Smith has only one afternoon to teach them. A problem arises when he teaches them too well; when Principal Wood arrives with the visitor, the students in the class are quick to point out her manners mistakes.

Concepts

The story encourages children to answer "Hello, how are you?" with "I am fine, thank you. How are you?" Also covered are shaking hands, looking at the speaker, taking turns to talk, not interrupting, speaking clearly, introducing people to each other, and introducing a new person to a group by name.

Read the Story: "Teaching the Principal a Lesson"

Reproduce the story found on pages 61–66. Staple the pages together in numerical order and read them to the class.

Guided Questions

1. According to Principal Wood, what is it like to walk into Mr. Smith's class?

2. What does the principal want Mr. Smith to teach his students?

3. When Mr. Smith says, "How are you, Mark?" what does Mark think he means?

4. What does Mark do when Mr. Smith tries to shake his hand?

5. When would it be appropriate to give someone a high five rather than a handshake?

6. Why does Carl whistle when Principal Wood introduces Mr. Grace?

7. Why does he whistle again when the principal is speaking?

8. After meeting them, what does Mr. Grace think of the students in Mr. Smith's class?

Role-Play Ideas

1. Act out someone new coming to play with an existing soccer team. First, show the introduction using incorrect manners; then, introduce the new player correctly.

2. Role-play a scene where one child is trying to explain something important and another child keeps interrupting her.

3. Practice meeting and greeting someone important; have students say, "Hello, how are you?" and "I'm fine, thank you. How are you?" while shaking hands.

Meet & Greet Manners

Hello.
My name is _____.
How are you?

Hello.
I'm _____.
I am fine, thank you.
It is nice to meet you.

Remember to also:
Shake hands.
Look people in the eye.

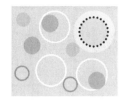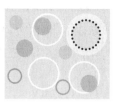

Teaching the Principal a Lesson

Mr. Smith loved his class. They were enthusiastic. They were funny. They were kind. But, he had to admit, there was a problem. He wasn't surprised when Mrs. Wood, the principal, called him into her office.

"Mr. Smith, you are a wonderful teacher. Your students always do so well. . . ." She paused.

"I know what you're going to say, Mrs. Wood."

"You do?"

"I think so."

"Go on then," said the principal.

"My students are rude."

"That's it! Walking into your classroom is like entering a friendly, overcrowded zoo!"

"They don't mean to be rude. They get so excited, they forget their manners."

"Well, I have a challenge for you, Mr. Smith. Tomorrow, your class will have an important visitor. His name is Mr. Grace, and his grandmother founded the school 73 years ago."

"Can't he visit a different class?" asked Mr. Smith.

"No. When his grandmother founded the school, he was in second grade. He especially wants to visit the second grade."

"Oh dear," said Mr. Smith.

"I'm sure you can turn them around."

"In one afternoon?" said a very worried Mr. Smith.

"It's all the time you have," said Mrs. Wood.

Back in class, Mr. Smith explained to his students that they were going to meet and greet a special visitor. It was important that they be polite, so they were going to spend the afternoon practicing their manners.

"Mark," he said to the boy who needed to practice most, "you and I are going to start. Come and stand with me." Once Mark was at the front of the room, Mr. Smith looked him in the eye and smiled.

"Hello, how are you, Mark?"

Mark looked confused, "Mark is the name my mom gave me."

"No! Not how are you named Mark—but, Mark, how are you?"

Mark still looked confused. Mr. Smith tried to stay patient.

"Just say, 'I am very well, thank you.' Then, you ask me the same thing."

Mark looked up at Mr. Smith. "I am very well, thank you. Um, how are you, Mark?"

"No!" said Mr. Smith, "I'm not Mark—you are. You need to say my name."

"Oh, sorry. How are you, Mr. Smith?"

"Very well, thank you." Mr. Smith put his hand out to shake Mark's. Mark gave him a high five.

"This is going to be a long afternoon," thought Mr. Smith.

But before long, the class got the hang of "Hello, how are you?" "I'm fine, thank you," and "How are you?" With another role-play, Mr. Smith taught them not to interrupt when someone is speaking.

Then, Mr. Smith tried to explain how to introduce a new person.

"Carl, Emma, Ben, and Sarah come to the front please. Emma, you're new. Carl, you introduce her to the others."

Emma left the room and came back in.

"Hi," Carl said. "Meet the gang."

"That won't do, Carl," said Mr. Smith. "She needs names, and you need her name. Try again."

"Hi, I'm Carl. What's your name?"

"Emma."

"Hi, Emma," said Carl. "This is Ben and Sarah."

"Hi, Emma. It is nice to meet you," Ben and Sarah said.

"Hooray!" said Mr. Smith. "All right! Now, get into groups of three. Two of you role-play the things we have talked about; the third person watches. If someone gets something wrong, the watcher should whistle."

The children practiced saying, "Hello, how are you?" "I'm fine, thank you. How are you?" and "It is nice to meet you." They shook hands, introduced each other, and tried to remember not to interrupt. And, they whistled a lot.

The next morning, Mr. Smith said, "I hope you've all been practicing." There was a knock at the door. "Come in," sang Mr. Smith in his nicest voice.

In came Principal Wood with an old man. "Meet Class Five," said Mrs. Wood to the visitor.

To Mr. Smith's horror, Carl whistled loudly.

"We need names, Mrs. Wood," said Carl indignantly. "We need to know his name, and he needs to know our names."

The principal looked at Mr. Smith.

"I'm sorry, Mrs. Wood. They are excited to meet our visitor and want to do everything properly. They want to be introduced by name."

"How charming," said the old man.

"Very well," said the principal. "This is Mr. Grace."

"Carl is going to introduce us," Mr. Smith said. Carl walked up to Mr. Grace and shook his hand.

"Hello, Mr. Grace, I'm Carl. It is nice to meet you." He turned to the rest of the class and said, "And, this is Ben, Sarah, Mark, Tom, Ahmad, Bella, Milo, Josh, Amy, Miguel, Tasha, . . . "

"Do we need everyone's name?" interrupted Principal Wood.

This time the whole class whistled!

Mr. Grace chuckled, "Mrs. Wood, I think you interrupted my friend."

Mrs. Wood was flustered, "Very well, Carl. I'm sorry. Please continue."

"This is Charlotte, Ruth, Isaac, Emma, Jamayla, Michael, Natalie, Sophie, Andrew, Juan, Paul, and Wesley."

"Nice to meet everyone," Mr. Grace said. "How are you all?" he smiled.

"Very well, thank you, sir," they all said, "and how are you, sir?"

"Charmed," he laughed. "Absolutely charmed. What a polite class you have, Mr. Smith."

"I do, don't I?" he said, winking at his students.

"Perhaps, you could teach some manners to Mrs. Wood?" Mr. Grace said. Mrs. Wood blushed.

The End

Unit 7
Good Sportsmanship

Story Summary

Baseball coach Bud Kunkle thought he knew everything there was to know about the game. What he didn't know is, that in Australia, there is a kangaroo baseball league. When Bud accepts the invitation to help the Sydney Furry Sox, he doesn't realize what he's letting himself in for. The kangaroos think that sticking to the rules will lose them games. They are shocked at Bud's suggestion that they would play better and enjoy the sport more if they respected it, followed the rules, and learned how to be good sports.

Concepts

This story and the activities below encourage children to engage in sportsmanlike behavior: follow the rules, don't argue, be considerate of other players, be a graceful loser and congratulate the winner, be a graceful winner and compliment the loser, don't yell bad words, cheer but don't irritate, and be a considerate spectator.

Read the Story: "Kangaroo Baseball"

Reproduce the story found on pages 71–78 or print out the story pages in color using the CD found in the back cover of this book. Staple the pages together in numerical order and read them to the class.

Guided Questions

1. Why don't the kangaroos use baseball bats? What do they use instead?

2. Why is Bud horrified on his first day with the Sydney Furry Sox? What rules do they break?

3. What is the only rule the kangaroos play by?

4. Why do the kangaroos think they shouldn't have to play by the rules?

5. Why does Bud say it is important to respect the rules of a game?

6. Besides the rules of the game, Bud tells the team about the rules of good sportsmanship. What are they?

7. Bud also tells the team how their fans can behave in a sportsmanlike way. What does he say?

8. What are some of the things the Sydney Furry Sox fans do and say that will change if Bud gets his way?

Role-Play Ideas

1. A hard-fought baseball game is over. Role-play how the teams interact after the game. First, have students play the scene with gloating winners and pouting losers. Then, replay the scene with both teams demonstrating good sportsmanship.

2. Act out a bleacher full of fans during an exciting game. Show how the crowd can react to the events on the field while showing enthusiastic support for the athletes of both teams.

Be a Team Player

PLAY BY THE RULES!
1. Don't cheat. It is better to play fairly and lose than to win by cheating!

2. Don't argue. Remember to be considerate of the other players on your team.

DON'T YELL INSULTS OR BAD WORDS—EVER!
1. Don't yell insults at the players on your team when they mess up or make a mistake. Encourage them instead!

2. Don't yell insults at the players on the other team.

Be a Good Winner and a Good Loser

IF YOUR TEAM WINS . . .
1. Don't boast.

2. Don't make the losing team feel bad.

3. Always shake hands with the losing team and say "well done."

IF YOUR TEAM LOSES . . .
1. Shake hands and say "well done" to the winning team.

Be a Good Fan

BE A GOOD FAN . . .

1. Cheer on your team.

2. Be encouraging!

3. Don't yell insults or bad words at anyone!

Kangaroo Baseball

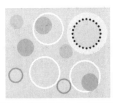
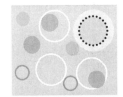

Baseball coach Bud Kunkle knew just about everything there was to know about baseball. But, he didn't know about kangaroo baseball. That's not surprising—it is a well kept secret. Not only is baseball an American sport, as we all know, and kangaroos are Australian, but they are embarrassed about their playing style. With such short arms, holding a bat is tricky. So, they use their own built-in bats, which are stronger, longer, and easier to hold on to—their tails! It looks strange to see a ball pitched to the back end of a kangaroo, but they can really hit that ball!

The kangaroo baseball league had always kept to itself, but when the Sydney Furry Sox lost every game last season, they were desperate. They decided that they needed to hire a human baseball coach and contacted Bud. Bud had always wanted to go to Australia, so he said yes, not knowing what he was getting himself into.

On day one, Bud put the kangaroos into teams to watch them play. Bud was horrified—this wasn't baseball! The kangaroos were breaking every rule! Kangaroos hopping from base to base were tripped. In the field, if a kangaroo caught the ball, another player knocked the ball out of his paws. Kangaroo pitchers aimed and threw the ball at the batter's stomach. The kangaroos had one rule—that rule was to win.

Bud ran out onto the field. The kangaroos were surprised and stopped playing.

"Guys! Do you even know the rules of baseball?"

"We used to," said Joe, the kangaroo captain. He wiped his sweaty head with his paw. "But, nobody obeys them anymore. Why should we?"

"You'll ruin the game!" said Bud. "In a few years, no one will even know you're playing baseball. It's a great game—respect it! Play by the rules."

"But, what if that means we lose?" said Mickey, a small, strong kangaroo, who was tapping his tail on the ground.

"You have to practice, try your best, and win without cheating."

"Not cheat?" said Joe. "Next, you'll say don't trip a guy up if he's going to get a home run, or don't knock the ball out of a kangaroo's paw when he's going to tag us out."

"You bet I'm going to tell you that, you ridiculous animals! Carry on like this, and it won't be baseball! It will just be a big fight!"

The kangaroos looked thoughtful. Mickey scratched his white stomach.

"Rules don't matter," he said. "Just get those home runs in. That's what makes us feel good, isn't it fellas?"

The kangaroos nodded and thumped their tails.

"It feels even better," said Bud, "when you respect the rules and still win."

The kangaroos were quiet, imagining what that would be like. Joe turned to Bud. "I guess you'll have to remind us about the rules."

After spending the morning learning the rules of the game of baseball, the kangaroos wanted to get out, run around, and hit some balls. Bud decided to set up a practice game. At first, he was pleased to see that the kangaroos were sticking to the rules. But, about 10 minutes into the game, another problem came to light. Mickey made a great hit. But, the ball fell from the sky and was caught by a kangaroo named Bruce.

"You batted it straight into his paws, you idiot!" yelled one of the kangaroos.

"You're going to lose us the game, dimwit!" shouted another.

"No no no!" shouted Bud.

An angry kangaroo called Skippy waved the rules in Bud's face. "Show me where it says we can't shout at him for making a stupid mistake."

"The rules of sportsmanship aren't written down! Don't tell me," said Bud, "you haven't heard of them."

"Nope," said Joe.

"We need to go to college to learn all of this!" said Skippy.

"What are the rules of sportsmanship, Bud?" said Joe.

"For a start, don't yell insults at your team's players when they mess up or at players on the other team."

"No hollering?" said Bruce.

"Sure, you can holler. Holler words like 'well done' or 'good try' or 'never mind,'" answered Bud.

The kangaroos laughed, until they saw Bud wasn't joking.

Joe scratched his floppy ear. "Anything else?"

"Yes," said Bud. "If you win, don't boast or make the losers feel . . ."

"Like losers?" said Bruce.

"Yes."

"What about our song?" said Joe. He began to sing. "We're better than you. We're better than you. You'll never beat us, whoopdee-doopdee-doo."

"That will have to go," said Bud with his hands on his hips.

Bud continued, "Oh, and another thing—if you lose, shake paws and say 'well done.'"

The kangas looked astonished. "We can't kick or hit them?" one said.

"No!" said Bud.

"That's gonna be hard," said Skippy.

"Hang on a minute!" said Bruce. "You mean to say that if we lose, we have to be nice to the winners?"

"Yes, sir. You will shake paws with them and say 'well done.'"

"For beating us?"

"That's right. Your fans will respect you."

"They will?"

"Yes, they will. Playing the game well is as important as winning."

The kangaroos stood in silence, their tails flat on the ground behind them.

"You know what I'm worried about?" said Joe quietly.

"What?" asked Bud.

"Our fans aren't going to like this! They'll throw icky food at us."

"Your fans throw food?" Bud said.

"Sure they do. They throw fruit, leftover supper, sour milk . . ."

"They sing songs too," said Mickey, and then he sang, "You won't win; you're gonna fail. You'll never hit that ball with your weedy tail."

"That's got to stop too," said Bud.

"Fans won't come if they have to sit in silence!" said Skippy.

"They can cheer you on, but they can't yell rude things about the other team or the other fans, and they can't throw things!"

'Well, who'd have thought it, fellas?" said Joe, putting his paw on Bud's shoulder. "It's going to be a whole new game."

The End

Unit 8
Out & About in Public

Story Summary

When Amy finally gets the puppy she's longed for, she discovers what hard work training him is. Hector is so badly behaved that Amy's family can't take him out in public. This makes Amy sad and upset. Then, when visiting a farmers' market and some stores with her parents, Amy also forgets the rules of how to behave when you're out and about. The next day, she takes Hector to his obedience training class for puppies and is given a taste of her own medicine when Hector makes the same mistakes that she made the day before.

Concepts

The story emphasizes rules to follow when out in public: Stay by parents, teachers, or caregivers; do not run off. Remember to say "please" and "thank you." Do not beg for things. Do not touch things without asking. If lost inside a store, movie, or restaurant, look for a person who works there (usually identified by a name tag or uniform). If lost outside, such as at a park, stay put and your parents or caregivers will find you. Do not leave with anyone else.

Read the Story: "A Disastrous Day Out"

Reproduce the story found on pages 83–88. Staple the pages together in numerical order and read them to the class.

Guided Questions

1. Why don't Amy's parents let her take Hector when they go to the farmers' market?

2. What is the first mistake that Amy makes once they are at the market?

3. How does the man selling hot chocolate react to her behavior?

4. What big—and possibly dangerous—mistake does Amy make next?

5. Why is this never a good thing to do?

6. Why does a store assistant have to say "Young lady!" to Amy?

7. Describe the two things that Amy does remember how to do correctly: what to do if you are lost inside and what to do if you are lost outside.

8. What does Hector do the next night at puppy training class that is similar to Amy's behavior at the farmers' market?

Role-Play Ideas

1. Role-play a scene in which a child is lost in a shopping mall. Because the child forgets what she is supposed to do, the situation worsens, and she is even harder to find.

2. Pair students to act out a scene in which one child pretends to be a stranger trying to convince the other child to go with him. The "stranger" should be persistent, but the child must not give in. Talk about what words and actions were effective.

3. Have a group of three children role-play a scene in which two of the children are parents and one is their young child. The family goes into a store, and the child doesn't use good out-and-about manners. Have the parents explain how she can correct her behavior.

How to Behave When Out & About in Public

1. Stay by your parents, teacher, or caregiver with whom you are out with in public.

2. Remember to say "please" and "thank you" to the people who work at the places you visit, such as restaurants, stores, libraries, or zoos. Be polite!

3. Do not beg or cry for things that you want. You will only embarrass yourself.

4. Do not touch things in stores or other public places without asking first.

What to Do If You Are Lost — Out & About Inside

2. Find a person wearing a uniform or a name tag who works at the place where you are. Tell the person that you are lost. This person will make an announcement for your parents or caregiver to come to where you are.

1. Stay by your parents, teacher, or any caregiver with whom you are out in public with and you won't get lost.

3. Never walk outside of the store or place where you are lost with a stranger. **STAY IN THE BUILDING.**

What to Do If You Are Lost — Out & About Outside

2. Find a person wearing a uniform, security uniform, or name tag who works at the park, zoo, or amusement park where you are. Tell the person that you are lost. This person will make an announcement for your parents or caregiver to come to where you are.

1. Stay by your parents, teacher or any caregiver with whom you are out in public with and you won't get lost.

3. NEVER walk away with a stranger—even a friendly-looking person. Wait for your parents to come and find you. STAY PUT.

A Disastrous Day Out

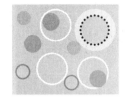
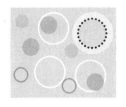

As soon as she was old enough to say the word "puppy," Amy wanted to have one. For birthdays and Christmas, it was the only thing she asked for. Her parents hadn't said yes because they both worked. The puppy would be on its own all day. But, when Amy's father left his job to work from home, they decided that Amy, who was now seven, could have her own puppy. She chose a darling black cocker spaniel and named him Hector.

Amy took Hector to puppy training classes. He wasn't very good at doing what he was told. He nibbled shoes, jumped on people's laps, and ran between their legs and tripped them. He wouldn't come when he was called, and he chased after other dogs. The trainer said not to worry; Hector was young and would soon learn to behave.

One fall weekend, Amy and her parents were going downtown to the farmers' market in the park and a nearby area of stores. Amy wanted to take Hector.

"Not yet," her dad said. "We will bring him along once he learns how to behave. There will be lots of people there, and it will get dark early. With Hector's black coat, we could lose him outside."

"We couldn't take him into the farmers' market because he'd knock things down and eat any food that he could reach. It would be a nightmare," said Mom.

Amy was disappointed because she loved taking Hector outside. She just wished he would learn to behave a little faster.

As they were walking toward the market, Amy saw a hot chocolate stand.

"Can I have some hot chocolate?" she asked.

"After we're done shopping in that store," said her mom.

Amy was tired of her parents saying no. She stood in front of the vendor. "But, I want one right now!" The man selling the hot chocolate looked at Amy and then at her parents. He seemed embarrassed.

"No, Amy," said her dad. "We said later." Then, he turned to the man at the stand. "I'm sorry about this."

Amy felt silly. She backed away, not wanting to look at anyone. Suddenly, she saw her friend Claire, who was walking by some farmers' market stands. Amy started to run.

"Hey, Claire! Wait for me!" yelled Amy.

"Amy! Come back here!" called her mom, but Amy was too busy running and didn't hear her mom calling.

Amy watched as Claire disappeared through the doors of a store and was swallowed up into the noise and crowd.

Amy followed her into the store. Claire had to be in there somewhere! The store was packed with grown-ups, children, strollers, and rows and rows of things for sale. Claire was nowhere to be seen. Then, Amy noticed a huge display in the center of the store. Its beautiful decorations looked like fruit. She walked up to one of the arrangements and pinched a strawberry. Then, she squeezed an orange. They were a little bit soft, but she couldn't figure out what they were made of. She licked her finger and wiped it on the fruit. Then, she licked her finger again to see if she could taste anything.

"Young lady!" exclaimed a store clerk.

Amy looked up and saw the clerk frowning at her.

Amy ducked away from the store clerk, but then she couldn't find the door she had come in. It was dark outside. She couldn't see her parents or her friend Claire. Amy felt afraid and was ashamed of her behavior.

Suddenly, she remembered what her parents had taught her. They said if she was ever lost in a store, she should find someone who worked there. People who work in stores wear uniforms or name tags.

Amy spotted someone with a name tag on her shirt. "Excuse me," she said, "but I've lost my parents."

Very quickly, the store employee made an announcement over the loud speakers. Amy's parents arrived soon after. Amy cried from relief when she saw them. "I'm sorry," she said, when they were alone.

"Amy, we were scared! We were looking outside for you. We were lucky that we even heard the store announcement! Do you remember what we taught you to do if you were lost outside and not in a store?"

"Yes," Amy said, "I'd have stayed where I was and waited for you to find me. And, I wouldn't have gone off with anyone I didn't know."

"At least you remembered to go to a store employee for help," said her dad as they walked home across the park. "You're as bad as Hector."

The next day, Amy and her dad came home from puppy training with Hector. They were laughing as they came through the door.

"What's so funny?" asked Amy's mom.

"Hector gave Amy a taste of her own medicine tonight."

"What happened?"

"He took off in the parking lot," said Amy, "and wouldn't come back. He ran up to a man eating a hamburger and looked at him with his big eyes. Then, he jumped up and grabbed the burger right out of the man's hand!"

"How did that make you feel, Amy?" asked her mom.

"Awful! First, I was worried he'd get hurt. Then, I was embarrassed that he stole someone's hamburger. Dad had to buy the man another one!"

Amy's mom looked down at Hector. He wagged his tail.

"Well, the sooner you two both learn to behave, the sooner we can go out and have some fun."

Amy sat on the floor. Hector jumped into her lap and licked her face.

"What a pair!" said Dad.

The End

Story Summary

For once, Tom is really pleased to do his homework. His assignment is to pretend he is an alien visiting Earth for the weekend. After returning to his home planet, he must write a report about what is important to human beings. Tom watches his sister as she has a misunderstanding and then makes up with a friend, he observes his mom bake a pie to take to an elderly person who is sick and lonely, and he notices that his mom obeys the rules of the road when she is driving. Tom concludes that the most important thing to humans is other humans and that rules and laws are made for protection and fairness.

Concepts

The story encourages children to think about being good family members, friends, neighbors, and students, and it conveys why it is good to follow the rules of home, school, and country.

Read the Story: "Dakob's Homework"

Reproduce the story found on pages 91–98. Staple the pages together in numerical order and read them to the class.

Guided Questions

1. Why is Tom happy with this particular piece of homework? What does he like to do?

2. What does Lucy say that nobody likes to have happen? What other things can you think of that people would not want to have happen to them? (*being gossiped about*, *being treated unfairly*)

3. When Tom asks Lucy and Nora why they are hugging each other, they just laugh because it seems like a silly question. But, why do people hug each other?

4. Tom's mom explains the purpose of rules and laws. What does she say they do?

5. What does Tom decide is the most important thing to human beings?

6. Do you think everyone would agree with Tom's conclusion? What are some other things he might have noticed as being really important to humans?

7. Tom says in his report that he saw three different groups of humans. What are they?

8. Why does Tom say there have to be rules in schools?

Role-Play Ideas

1. Role-play a scene where someone is not a good neighbor. Then, repeat the scene, this time with the person showing what it is to be a good neighbor.

2. Create a scenario where one child is in charge of the country for the day. The child can make up a new law—it can be quite silly—that everyone has to obey. Role-play the scene where the new law is announced. What do people say about it?

3. Imagine a school with no rules at all. Role-play a teacher trying to teach a classroom lesson in this school. Discuss the difficulties students would face when trying to learn.

Be a Good Citizen

People Are Citizens of Many Groups

Citizens of their families

Citizens of their classrooms

Citizens of their communities

Citizens of their countries

Every citizen has the responsibility to
follow the rules and **obey the laws** and to
respect authority and **contribute to the group**.
Rules and laws were created to protect people and to make sure
that they are as safe and happy as they can be.

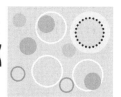
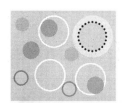

"Quiet, everyone," said Miss Mack to Class Five. "You need to write down the homework assignment for this weekend. I want you to imagine that you are from outer space. You know nothing at all about planet Earth. You have been asked to spend two days here watching people. When you return to your home planet, you must write a report on what you learned about the people on Earth during your visit. The title of the report is 'What Is Important to Human Beings.' Your homework assignment is to write that report."

Tom didn't usually enjoy homework, but he was excited about this assignment. He loved stories and movies about space travel and aliens. He liked the idea of really trying to imagine what it would be like to arrive on Earth, knowing absolutely nothing about it.

So that weekend, Tom kept a small notebook in his pocket and pretended he was an alien. In his imagination, Tom was bright blue. He had three eyes, six legs, and one very powerful ear. He came from a small planet called Zogadog and his name was Dakob.

Tom's sister, Lucy, and his mom and his dad went about their business as usual. They were used to Tom playing make-believe games and pretending to be someone else.

On Saturday morning, Lucy came into the den looking sad. Tom sat next to her on the couch and got out his notebook.

"Why-is-there-water-coming-out-of-your-eyes?" he said in a strange, alien voice.

"Nora's going to the mall with Alice, and they didn't ask me to come."

"Why-does-that-make-you-unhappy?" Tom said in the same weird voice.

"Because no one likes to be left out!" Lucy said, starting to cry again.

Then, the doorbell rang. Lucy went to the door. It was Nora.

"Sorry I didn't invite you to the mall," Nora said to Lucy. "I wanted to get you back because you didn't invite me to go bowling last week. But, I hate the thought of you being upset, so I came back to ask you to come too."

Lucy's face broke into a huge smile, and they hugged each other. "I'm sorry too," said Lucy.

Tom stood next to the hugging girls. "Why-do-you-squeeze-each-other?" he said.

Both girls looked at him and laughed.

In the kitchen, his mom was cooking something.

"Why-are-you-covering-white-wet-lumps-with-white-dusty-stuff?"

"I'm making an apple pie for Mrs. Cross. She's been sick and hasn't left her house all week. I'm going to drive it over and visit with her awhile. She's lonely."

Tom's mom was so used to his funny ways, she didn't even ask him why he was talking strangely and scribbling notes in a little book.

"Do you want to come with me?" she said. "Mrs. Cross would love to see you."

In the car Tom noticed his mom checking the speedometer. "Why-did-you-slow-down?"

"The speed limit changed. I was going too fast."

"But-you-said-we-had-to-be-quick."

"Being in a hurry isn't as important as driving safely." She glanced down at Tom, writing away in his notebook. "Rules and laws are made so that as many people as possible can be safe. You know that, Tom."

"I-am-not-Tom. I-am-Dakob-and-I-come-from-planet-Zogadog."

"Oh sorry," said Tom's mom. "For a moment, I thought you were my son, Tom. My mistake."

"That-is-all-right," said Tom.

"Rules in school or laws for the whole country are there to protect people," she explained. "Laws are to make sure everyone is as safe and happy as they can be."

Tom spent the whole weekend talking in a funny voice, wearing his alien costume, asking strange questions, and writing in his notebook. He watched the news and read the newspapers. On Sunday night, he wrote his report.

"'What Is Important to Human Beings,' by Dakob, Planet Zogadog.

"After my weekend on planet Earth, I have found out what matters to human beings. The answer is very simple: other human beings. Human beings believe that all other human beings matter.

"On Earth, I found out about three different human groups: families (the smallest groups of humans), schools (where little humans go to learn about the world and themselves), and workplaces (where big humans go every day to do their jobs).

"In families, humans are close and they touch and squeeze each other."

"In schools, there are things called rules. Young humans have to do what they are told. Sometimes they don't like this, but it is so that they can learn as much as possible and everyone is safe."

"In workplaces, there aren't as many rules as at school, but there are always some. The rules are different in different places and for different jobs, but rules are always there to help people do their jobs well, to keep people safe, and to make things fair for everyone. Rules that are for everyone in a country are called laws, and it's very serious to ignore them."

"Rules and laws are the way humans look after each other. They are Earth's way of showing that everybody matters."

Tom got an A on his report and read it to the whole school at an assembly. He even used his funny alien voice.

The End

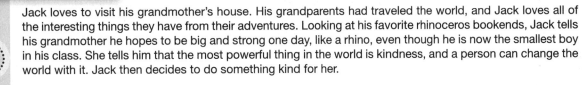

Unit 10
Learning to Be Kind

Story Summary

Jack loves to visit his grandmother's house. His grandparents had traveled the world, and Jack loves all of the interesting things they have from their adventures. Looking at his favorite rhinoceros bookends, Jack tells his grandmother he hopes to be big and strong one day, like a rhino, even though he is now the smallest boy in his class. She tells him that the most powerful thing in the world is kindness, and a person can change the world with it. Jack then decides to do something kind for her.

Concepts

This story looks at what a powerful force kindness is and encourages children to understand that they can make a great impact on the world by being kind and considerate. The guided questions below help students recognize that in order to be kind, they need to understand and empathize with others.

Read the Story: "Powerful Stuff"

Reproduce the story found on pages 101–106. Staple the pages together in numerical order and read them to the class.

Guided Questions

1. What is it about the rhinoceros that Jack envies?

2. Why, according to Jack's grandmother, is kindness such a powerful thing?

3. What act of kindness did Jack's grandfather like to do? What made him chuckle?

4. Jack remembers an act of kindness from his first day at school. Who showed kindness and what was the lasting effect of that person's actions?

5. Name an act of kindness that another person has done for you.

6. How does Jack know his grandmother likes what he did for her?

7. In order to be kind, what skills or traits does a person need? (*being aware of what people are thinking and feeling, being empathetic, feeling compassion*)

8. Think of some acts of kindness you can do today. Then, follow through. How do you think your actions will impact others?

Role-Play Ideas

1. Role-play a situation where someone unexpectedly does something very kind for a stranger. The scene can be funny or serious.

2. When someone is kind to a person, it can make the person want to be kind to others. Act out a scene in which someone is kind to someone else, and then show that person doing something kind for another person. Continue the chain reaction so that there is a long line of kindnesses.

3. Just as being kind can be "catching," so can being rude or mean. Repeat the scenario above, but show how one person's unkindness can lead to another unkind action.

Who Is Kind?

People show kindness through words and actions.
Look at the pictures. Color the ☺ if the child is "being kind."
Color the ☹ if the child is "not being kind."

Powerful Stuff

Jack was visiting his grandmother. He loved her house; it was big and had lots of interesting objects in it from when his grandparents traveled around the world. His favorite things were the heavy black bookends from South Africa that were shaped like rhinoceroses. He also loved the set of kettle drums from Jamaica and the big piece of jagged coral from Australia. The huge, floppy sombrero from Mexico was pretty cool, too.

Every time he visited, Jack looked at these things. His grandmother never told him not to touch them or worried he might damage them. She always laughed when he put the sombrero on his head. It almost covered his whole face.

Grandmother wanted Jack to enjoy all of these things that were precious to her. She loved to tell him stories about her travels. Jack's grandfather had died before Jack was born, but Jack felt he knew him from his grandmother's stories. Jack was sure that he and his grandfather would have been very good friends.

Today, Jack was looking at one of the rhino bookends. He stroked its strong legs and then put his finger on the tip of its horn.

"Do you think this is one of the strongest animals in the world?" he asked his grandmother.

"I don't know," she said. "Hippos are very strong too, and elephants must be pretty powerful!"

"I wish I was strong," said Jack, who was the smallest boy in his class. "When I'm 16, I'm going to work out at the gym to get muscles as big as this rhino's."

"You don't have to wait until you're 16 to be powerful, Jack."

Jack was interested. "I don't?" He sat next to Grandmother on the sofa.

"Anyone, big or small, can do the most powerful thing on earth."

"What's that?" Jack was really interested now.

"Be kind." She smiled at him.

Jack was disappointed. "That's not powerful like a rhino."

"No, but being kind is a much stronger kind of powerful."

"How?" asked Jack.

"You can change someone's world with it, Jack. Don't you think that's powerful? I promise you, no one forgets an act of kindness."

"I suppose so," he said. "I've just never thought about it like that."

"Do you know what your grandfather used to love to do?" Grandmother smiled, as she always did when she was remembering Grandfather.

"At the toll booth on the highway, he'd pay for the car behind him. He'd chuckle for miles at the thought of the people's faces when the booth attendant said the car in front had paid for them."

Jack suddenly remembered his first day of school. He'd been lost and scared. An older kid, who Jack thought looked scary, had asked which class Jack was looking for, and the older kid took Jack all the way to his classroom.

"Whenever I saw that boy, I felt grateful," he said to his grandmother. "It was as if we had a special something between us."

"Jack, maybe one day you will grow up to be strong. You can go to the gym and have rhino muscles. You might be able to lift weights, win competitions, and look after yourself in danger. But always remember, the biggest muscles on Earth can't change someone's world like an act of kindness can. You can start changing the world today."

Jack gave his grandmother a hug and then said good-bye. All the way home he thought about what she said.

The next day, Jack decided to do something kind for his grandmother. He asked his mom to get out her old pictures. He found a photo of his grandfather when he was young. He was laughing in the picture. Jack took all of the money he had saved and bought a beautiful picture frame.

He took the framed picture to her house. "This is for you, Grandmother." She held the picture in her hands.

"I know you think of him a lot, and you still miss him. I picked this picture because it reminds me of him laughing when he paid for the car behind him at the toll booth."

Jack's grandmother didn't say anything. She didn't need to. Her face changed and her eyes filled up. She hugged him really hard. He knew his act of kindness had worked its magic.

The End

Unit 11
Learning to Be Fair

Story Summary

It's the first day of George and his family's much-anticipated Disney holiday. There with his parents, brother, and sister, George gets angry because they aren't going to Epcot, his first choice, until the second day. He stomps off and leaves the rest of the family to work out how to deal with his selfish behavior. When George returns, they tell him he can make all of the decisions for the rest of the vacation. He quickly realizes that he wouldn't enjoy that because it would be so unfair. George concludes that it is not just what he wants that matters.

Concepts

The story encourages children to think about sharing, taking turns, cooperating, and taking other people's wishes and ideas into consideration. Many children exclaim, "That's not fair!" when they believe that they have been deprived of something they wanted or had expected to receive. Help children develop a realistic understanding of "fairness" by:

- being consistent;
- creating clear expectations;
- teaching that certain rights come with age or maturity;
- helping children distinguish between accidental and intentional actions; and
- assisting children in learning how to share, take turns, listen, and not overreact.

Read the Story: "Me Me Me!"

Reproduce the story found on pages 109–114. Staple the pages together in numerical order and read them to the class.

Guided Questions

1. What is the first thing that happens in this story that tells you George might not behave fairly towards his brother?

2. What upsets George on the first morning of their vacation?

3. Why does Ellen say he shouldn't complain about it?

4. Does George listen to what Ellen says? How does he handle his disappointment?

5. What does his family tell George he can do for the rest of the vacation?

6. How does George feel when they tell him their plan?

7. In order to be fair to everyone in a group of people, what has to happen? How do the people need to act? (*people need to be patient, take turns, and see other people's points of view*)

8. How do your teacher and classmates help to make your classroom a fair place to be? Are there ways to make your classroom even more fair?

Role-Play Ideas

1. Role-play a family scene in which one person in the family gets to decide everything. Then, act out the scene again with everyone having a say.

2. Imagine a teacher who is really unfair. Role-play a lesson in this teacher's class. (You might like to make the scene funny.)

3. Act out a group of friends arguing about what movie they will go to see. Have the players work out their differences so that by the end of the scene, they have cooperated and everyone is happy.

Poster Directions: Trace six stars onto aluminum foil. Glue the foil onto card stock. Let dry and cut out the stars. Read the statements. Glue a star to each statement that the children vote on as being "fair."

Fair or Not Fair?

There is only one cookie.
The kids cut it in two and shared it.
Is that fair?

Sam is four years old. His bedtime is 8:00.
His brother Tom is 10 years old.
Tom gets to stay up until 9:00.
Is that fair?

1.

2.

Ann bumped into Emma and caused her to drop her books.
Emma is mad at Ann.
Is that fair?

The class voted that Kate would be the line leader for the day.
But, Ian wanted to be the line leader.
Ian is upset with Kate. Is that fair?

3.

4.

Sara said that she would come over to Allie's house to play.
Sara never came or even called Allie.
Allie is upset with Sara. Is that fair?

Tim got a new baseball for his birthday.
Jon wanted a new baseball.
Now, Jon is mad at Tim.
Is that fair?

5.

6.

Me Me Me!

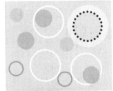
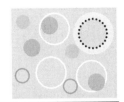

George woke up. He looked around. For a moment, he didn't know where he was. Then, he saw the Mickey Mouse wallpaper and he remembered! He was in Florida, and it was the first day of his family's Disney vacation.

George was there with his mom and dad, his older sister, Ellen, and his younger brother, Matt. The family had been planning and looking forward to this trip for two years.

The hotel apartment was fantastic. There was a pool and great big floating toys. There was an enormous TV, and each bedroom was decorated with a Disney character. George had picked the Mickey Mouse room, although there had been a bit of an argument because Matt had wanted to sleep there, too. Eventually, Matt agreed to sleep in the Winnie the Pooh room, and Ellen chose the Little Mermaid room.

At breakfast their dad told them the plans for the day.

"Today, we're going to the Magic Kingdom."

Ellen whooped, she was so excited. That was the place she most wanted to visit.

"But, I want to go to Epcot," said George.

"We're going to Epcot tomorrow, George," his mom said, pouring everyone some orange juice.

"But, I want to go today!" George pushed the glass away. A bit of juice spilled onto the table.

"We can't go there today" said his mom. "We've already bought our tickets. Come on, George. This time tomorrow, we'll be off to Epcot."

"It's not fair!" he said. "Ellen always gets her way."

"No, I don't!" Ellen said. "Besides, it's not like you won't get to go there at all—just not today."

Maybe George was just tired from all the traveling they had done the day before, but he was really grumpy.

"This is a stupid vacation, and I wish we hadn't come!" He ran back to his room.

The rest of the family looked at each other, disappointed that their first meal had ended with George running off angry.

"What are we going to do with him?" said George's dad.

"I have an idea," said Mom.

"Go and get him, Matt," Mom said after she told the rest of the family her idea, and they had practiced what they were going to say.

George came slowly down the stairs, glaring at everyone.

"Come here, George," said Dad. "We've got something to tell you."

George slumped in his chair and looked at the floor.

"We'll go to Epcot today, even though we'll have to buy new tickets, and it will cost us a lot of money," said Mom. "After all, the only thing that matters is that you are happy, George."

"Thanks, everybody," he grinned.

"And, every day, you get to choose where we go," said Ellen. "We'll go wherever you want."

"And, you can choose each night which room you sleep in," said Matt. "The rest of us will do whatever you tell us."

"And, when we're out during the day," said Dad, "you can choose where we eat."

"And, when we eat," said Mom.

"And, how long we stay at the park," said Ellen.

"And, you can decide which channel we watch on the TV," said Dad.

George looked at them. He should have felt happy about what they were saying, but it gave him a strange feeling in his stomach.

"I . . . I don't think I'd like that," he said.

"Why not?" said Mom, pretending to look surprised.

"It wouldn't be fair to the rest of you," said George.

"But, you'll get your own way for the whole vacation. Isn't that exactly what you want?" asked Dad.

"No," said George. "I couldn't really enjoy anything if I knew I was the only one who wanted to do it."

George's dad put his arm on his shoulder. "Right. How many of us are in this family, George?"

"Five," he replied.

"So, how many people matter?" asked Mom.

"Five," said George.

"That's right," said Mom.

"So, we're going to the Magic Kingdom today and Epcot tomorrow, right, George?" said Dad.

"Right," he said.

"And, Typhoon Lagoon the day after that, right?" said Matt hopefully.

"And, Typhoon Lagoon the day after that, Matt," said Dad.

"Let's stop talking about it and go!" said Ellen, standing up and doing a funny, excited dance.

"All right!" shouted George, jumping up and joining in.

The End

Unit 12
Learning to Be Honest

Story Summary

Sara falls in love with a tiny set of keys she finds on the floor of her classroom. She slips them into her pencil case, but almost immediately feels guilty. Then, she finds out the keys really belong to Michael, a boy in her class. He is very upset that the keys are missing; his mother is ill in the hospital, and the keys are his reminder of her. Everybody starts to look for the keys. Sara feels dreadful. Mrs. Thompson says that if anyone has taken the keys, that person should put them on her desk during recess. As Sara returns the keys with relief, Michael sees her. She apologizes to him and he forgives her. She promises herself never again to take something that doesn't belong to her.

Concepts

The story encourages children to be truthful and demonstrates that behaving dishonestly does not make you happy, even if it gets you something you think you want.

Read the Story: "The Keys to Happiness"

Reproduce the story found on pages 119–126. Staple the pages together in numerical order and read them to the class.

Guided Questions

1. Did Sara plan to steal Michael's keys?

2. Once Sara has the keys hidden in her pencil case, how does she feel?

3. When everyone is looking for the keys, Sara feels lonely. Why do you think she feels like this?

4. Do you think it is a good idea for Mrs. Thompson to invite the thief to put the keys on her desk during recess, with no questions asked?

5. If you were Michael, what would you have said when you saw Sara returning the keys? What might have happened if Michael had not been so forgiving?

6. How do you think Sara felt that night when she got home?

7. If you ever feel tempted to steal something, how could you stop yourself?

8. When Sara is feeling guilty and ashamed, her face feels like it is burning up. What other emotions affect how our bodies feel? (*joy, fear, sadness, excitement*)

Role-Play Ideas

1. Role-play a scene in a candy store. One child sees a friend steal some candy. Have the child choose what to do. Does he tell the owner? Does he tell the friend to put the candy back? Does he tell his parents? Talk about what happens as each possible scenario plays out.

2. Act out a scene that shows a person behaving dishonestly, for example, copying from another student's paper during a test. Then, repeat the scene but show the person being honest.

3. Role-play the scene where Michael discovers Sara putting the keys on Mrs. Thompson's desk. However, this time pretend Michael is not so kind and forgiving.

Tell the Truth!

Everyone Makes Mistakes! Never Be Afraid to Tell the Truth!

The Honesty Bulletin Board

Everyone on this list:

- tells the truth

- is honest and trustworthy

- keeps his or her word

- would not take something without permission

Isabella

Jayden

Brandon

Mike

Mia

The Classroom Honesty Book

Draw a picture of the person that you trust.

I trust _____

_____

because _____

_____

_____

_____

_____ ●

The Keys to Happiness

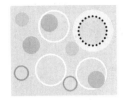
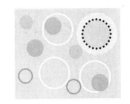
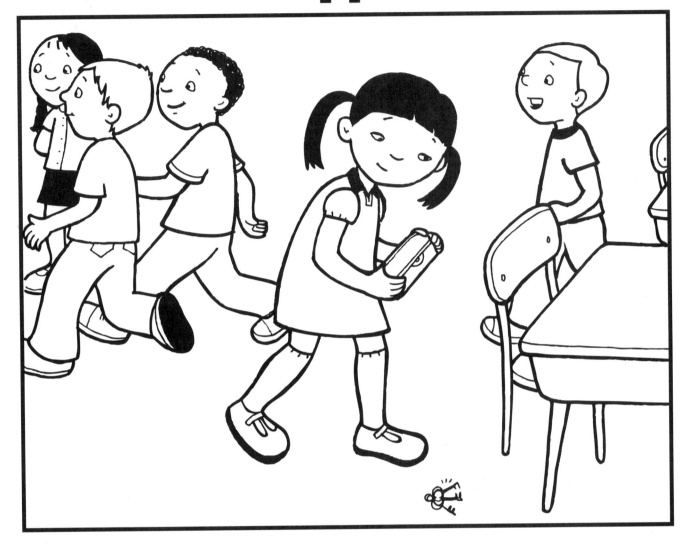

"Come and sit on the floor, everyone," said Mrs. Thompson. "We have 10 minutes until recess. We can read another chapter of our story if you're quick."

Sara went to her desk to put her pencil case away. That's when she saw them on the floor—a bunch of tiny, gleaming keys. Sara wasn't sure why she loved the look of them so much. The keys were small and yet fancy, with beautiful patterns on them.

Sara had never stolen anything (except maybe a cookie from her brother). She didn't think about what she was doing. One minute, she was thinking how gorgeous the keys looked, and the next, she was dropping them into her pencil case and putting the pencil case in her book bag.

Sara sat on the floor waiting for the rest of the class. An odd feeling stirred in her stomach. She loved the keys, but somehow it didn't feel good knowing they were in her bag.

"Hurry, everyone, or we won't have time to read the next chapter." Mrs. Thompson looked down at Sara and smiled. "Thanks for being so organized, Sara."

Sara smiled back. She liked Mrs. Thompson and tried to please her. Mrs. Thompson opened the book to the last page they had read. Then, she glanced up to see how many children were ready and sitting down. A look of concern crossed her face.

"Michael, what's the matter?"

Sara turned and saw Michael Kirby standing at the back of the room, crying. Michael's mom was in hospital, and he'd been upset in class a few times.

"What is it, Michael?" Mrs. Thompson said, going over to him.

"I've lost my mom's keys." He was crying harder now. "My mom and I take turns keeping them. They help us think about each other. I have them one day to think about her, and then she has them the next day to think about me."

"Don't worry, Michael. The keys must be here somewhere," said Mrs. Thompson. "What do they look like?"

"The keys are really small. They are from a suitcase that my grandmother got on her trip to Turkey. Those keys are 55 years old!" Big sobs shook Michael's shoulders up and down. "I'm supposed to give them back to my mom tonight. What will I say?"

Mrs. Thompson put her arm around his shoulders. "Michael, we'll find your keys. Won't we, everyone?"

The room had been silent. Everyone liked Michael and knew how upset he was that his mom was in hospital.

"Yes!" everyone said, and they all stood up and started looking.

Sara's face was burning up. It was painful to see Michael looking so upset and even more painful to know it was all her fault. As everyone hunted for the keys, Sara felt very lonely.

"They were here; I know they were," cried Michael, banging his fists on his own legs in frustration.

"All right, everybody," Mrs. Thompson said. "It makes me sad to even think about it, but maybe someone has taken Michael's keys. Maybe someone didn't realize how important they are." She looked at Michael and then back at the class. "But, now, all of you do know how important they are—that's for sure. It's time for recess. If anyone has the keys, make sure they are on my desk before we get back. No questions will be asked."

"Thank goodness," thought Sara. Mrs. Thompson had given her a way out.

When the bell rang, Sara said to her friends, "I'm going to the bathroom. I'll see you outside."

Sara ran back into the empty classroom. She got her bag and took out her pencil case. It felt so good to put the precious keys on Mrs. Thompson's desk.

"It was you!" Sara jumped. Michael was standing in the doorway. Sara felt hot and ashamed again.

"Michael, I'm so sorry!" she said, her voice cracking. "I saw them on the floor, and they were so . . . so . . . beautiful. I just picked them up without thinking. Please, forgive me, Michael. I didn't know they were special, but I still shouldn't have taken them."

Michael stood looking at her face. He walked to the desk and picked the keys up. He smiled a little bit. "They are beautiful, aren't they?"

"Really beautiful," she said.

Michael smiled. "Thanks for giving them back," he said. Sara wanted to hug him, she was so relieved, but she didn't want to embarrass him.

"Thank you for being kind about it, Michael. I really hope your mom gets better."

"Thanks," he said. "I miss her when she is in the hospital, but the game we play with the keys really does make me feel as if we're together. We both feel better."

"I've never stolen anything before." Sara's head was lowered. "Even before I knew they were yours, I felt bad. I wouldn't have enjoyed them."

"Michael, Sarah, is everything alright?" It was Mrs. Thompson.

"Yes, thank you," said Michael. "Look!" He held up the keys. "We found them!"

"Excellent!" said Mrs. Thompson.

Sara went out to play, promising herself that she would never, ever again take something that wasn't hers. It just wasn't worth it!

The End

Unit 13
Learning to Be Responsible

Story Summary

Emma is spending part of the summer living with her fussy Aunt Clarissa while her parents are in Thailand. When her aunt accuses her of not being responsible, Emma becomes upset. She doesn't know what the word means exactly, but she knows her aunt is angry. That night her aunt is taken seriously ill. Emma stays calm and calls 911. She asks the hospital to contact her parents in Thailand and call her best friend's parents so that she can stay with them while her aunt is in the hospital. Emma's mom returns, and they talk about being responsible not only in emergencies, but in day-to-day life. When her aunt comes to Emma's house to recuperate, Emma has the opportunity to prove how responsible she can be, and her aunt is grateful.

Concepts

This story and the activities below help children think about making good choices, knowing right from wrong, learning from mistakes, trying their hardest, caring for people and property, and picking up after themselves.

Read the Story: "Ice Cream & Ambulances"

Reproduce the story found on pages 131–136. Staple the pages together in numerical order and read them to the class.

Guided Questions

1. What word does Aunt Clarissa use to describe what she thinks Emma is not?

2. Emma finds the word *responsible* difficult to understand. What are some other words that have a similar meaning? (*able, accountable, capable, dependable, reliable, trustworthy*)

3. When Aunt Clarissa starts to feel ill, what does she believe is the cause?

4. What are three things that Aunt Clarissa is stricter about than Emma's parents?

5. When Emma calls 911, what does she remember to do so that the ambulance can come as quickly as possible?

6. Once Emma and Aunt Clarissa are at the hospital, what does Emma do?

7. Name two irresponsible things that Emma does. Then, name two responsible things.

8. Sometimes, Emma acts responsibly and sometimes she does not. Describe a time when you acted responsibly and a time when you didn't.

Role-Play Ideas

1. Role-play the following situation: Two friends find a wallet on the sidewalk. There is money in it. One friend wants to be responsible; the other doesn't. Act out their conversation. What happens in the end?

2. A few friends are playing in the yard with a ball. Someone kicks the ball, and it breaks a window next door. What should they do now? Role-play what would happen if they behaved irresponsibly. Then, repeat the scene with the friends behaving responsibly.

3. Have students imagine the scene where Aunt Clarissa asks Emma for her change from the trip to buy ice cream. Emma tells her aunt there isn't any money left over, and then Aunt Clarissa finds the ice cream melting on the kitchen floor. Act it out.

Learn Responsibility

• **Know right from wrong.**

• **Learn from your mistakes.**

• **Take care of people and property.**

• **Always try your hardest.**

• **Pick up after yourself.**

What Are You Responsible For?

What are your responsibilities at school?

What are your responsibilities at home?

What are your responsibilities to your friends?

Is It Responsible?

People often show responsibility through actions.
Look at the pictures.
Color the ☺ if the child is "being responsible."
Color the ☹ if the child is "not being responsible."

Jon forgot to feed his dog.

☺ ☹

1.

When Sara's family finished eating, she cleared the table.

☺ ☹

2.

It was garbage day, and Tim remembered to take out all of the garbage.

☺ ☹

3.

Becca helped her mother carry the groceries into the house.

☺ ☹

4.

Sam forgot to bring his homework back to school.

☺ ☹

5.

Katie only picked up her room when her mother reminded her.

☺ ☹

6.

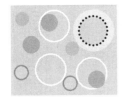 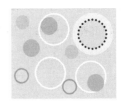

Story 13: Learning to Be Responsible
Ice Cream
& Ambulances

"The trouble with you," said Emma's Aunt Clarissa in a nasty, sharp voice, "is that you are not responsible."

"The trouble with you," Emma replied matching her aunt's tone, "is that you use words I don't understand!"

"You don't know what responsible means?" Aunt Clarissa looked horrified.

"No!" said Emma. "And, don't make me feel stupid because I've never heard of it."

Emma ran up the stairs and slammed her bedroom door. Aunt Clarissa sat on the sofa and shook her head.

Aunt Clarissa and Emma were spending part of the summer together. Emma's parents were in Thailand for a month. Aunt Clarissa was stricter than her parents about cleaning up, making her bed, and taking her shoes off when she came into the house. Emma knew she shouldn't argue with her aunt, but she felt grouchy and was missing her parents.

On the same night as their argument, Aunt Clarissa started to feel sick. "It's having to look after Emma," she thought. "It's too much for me."

She went to bed early, but by midnight, she knew she was really sick. She was burning up with a fever, she couldn't see properly, and she had a terrible headache. She was scared because she didn't know what was happening to her.

"Emma!" she called out. "Emma, come and help me."

At first, Emma thought she was dreaming. Then, she realized her aunt really was calling her. She ran to her bedroom. Her aunt's face was covered in sweat, and her skin looked as white as the sheets.

"What's the matter?" Emma asked.

"I don't know," her aunt replied, "but I need help." Then, Aunt Clarissa seemed to fall asleep, and Emma couldn't get her to wake up.

Emma went straight to the phone on the bedside table and called 911. Her heart was thumping, and her hands felt slippery on the telephone receiver.

Emma told the operator her name and Aunt Clarissa's address and explained what had happened to her aunt. Emma wanted to cry and to shout at them to come quickly, but she knew she had to be calm and speak clearly so that the 911 operator could understand her.

Emma rode to the hospital in the ambulance with her aunt. She held her hand and talked to her all the way, even though Emma didn't know if Aunt Clarissa could hear her.

The doctors said Aunt Clarissa needed an operation. Emma asked someone to call her parents in Thailand and then told the nurse the name and number of her best friend so that they could arrange for Emma to stay the night with them.

Two days later, Aunt Clarissa was still in hospital, and Emma's mom returned from Thailand.

They sat in the kitchen while Emma told her mom what had happened.

"Well done for being so responsible, Emma."

"That word is exactly what Aunt Clarissa said I wasn't on the day she got sick. We argued because I didn't know what it meant."

"Why? What had you done?" asked her mom.

"I'd gone to buy a carton of ice cream," said Emma. "I got the most expensive kind, so there wasn't any change to bring back. Then, I forgot to put the ice cream in the freezer, and it melted all over the kitchen floor."

"Oh dear," said her mom. "I can see why your aunt didn't like that."

"So, am I responsible or not?" said Emma, trying to understand.

"You were definitely responsible during the emergency. You knew the right people to call for help, and you did it very well. You saved your aunt's life, and I'm really, really proud of you."

"But, what about the ice cream?" questioned Emma.

"Well, spending all of your aunt's money on the most expensive kind of ice cream wasn't responsible. Neither was forgetting to put it in the freezer. You need to work on being as responsible all of the time as you were during the emergency."

"Seeing her so sick made me realize how much I love her, even though she can be kind of fussy," said Emma.

Aunt Clarissa did not have anyone to look after her. So, when she got out of hospital, she came to stay with Emma's family. Emma took her aunt meals and helped her walk up and down the stairs. She kept her company and took her books back and forth from the library.

One afternoon, Aunt Clarissa gave Emma a hug. "You did know what it means to be responsible. You saved my life. Thank you."

"Now, I'm trying to be responsible all of the time, not just when there is an emergency," said Emma.

"You are responsible and you are kind!"

"Oh, thank you, Aunt Clarissa!" said Emma, and they gave each other a huge hug.

The End

Unit 14
Learning to Be Respectful

Story Summary

Kate and Ben are neighbors and good friends. When Kate's mom asks if they will play with her boss's children, Roger and Rebecca, for a couple of hours, they agree. Roger and Rebecca tease Kate and Ben for being friends, read Kate's private journal, and are rude to Kate's mom. Finally, when Roger forgets to lock the bathroom door—and Rebecca forgets to knock—Roger is the one left feeling that a bit more respect would be in order.

Concepts

The story emphasizes the importance of expressing gratitude and showing respect for other people, their property, and their privacy.

Read the Story: "Nice Underpants!"

Reproduce the story found on pages 141–146. Staple the pages together in numerical order and read them to the class.

Guided Questions

1. What is the first thing that Roger and Rebecca ask when they are alone with Kate and Ben?

2. What do they do when Kate and Ben are in the kitchen getting cookies and juice?

3. Why shouldn't they have done this? In what other situations do you need to respect someone's privacy?

4. When Kate's mom comes in with more juice, what does Roger say when she steps between him and the TV?

5. What do you think he should have done or said in this situation? (*waited for her to move*, *said "excuse me," moved himself*)

6. What embarrassing thing happens with Roger and Rebecca?

7. Whose fault is it?

8. Go through the story again. Each time Roger or Rebecca is rude, say what he or she should have done or said to be respectful.

Role-Play Ideas

1. Act out the story, but this time have Roger and Rebecca behave respectfully.

2. Role-play a classroom scene where pupils are disrespectful to their teacher. Then, role-play the same scene with the students showing respect.

3. Have two students act out a scenario where a grumpy old man is quite rude, but the young person he speaks to manages to remain respectful.

Learn Respect

Treat others how you would like to be treated. Use manners. Share and take turns. Talk kindly.

Take care of property. Pick up after yourself.

Be kind to animals. Respect the Earth—never litter.

How Do You Show Respect?

**Draw two pictures of you
doing things that show respect.**

How Do You Rate?

Were you respectful today?

1. Did you listen? . . . .

2. Did you speak
   kindly to others? . . . .

3. Did you play fair? . . . .

4. Did you take turns? . . . . . .

5. Did you share? . . . .

6. Did you pick up
   after yourself? . . . .

7. Did you use magic
   words, such as *please*
   and *thank you?* . . . .

"Nice Underpants!"

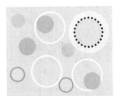
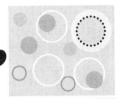

Kate and Ben were neighbors. They had been friends since they were babies. Now, they were eight. Their friendship worked well because they enjoyed the same things. They both liked soccer. They both liked baking cookies. They liked the same music. When they weren't together, they both liked to keep a journal. They had even bought journals as gifts for each other. Kate bought Ben one with a red leather cover and paper with gold edges. Ben bought Kate one with pages of handmade paper.

One day, Kate's mom came into the kitchen, where Kate and Ben were making cookies. "Would you two play with Roger and Rebecca this afternoon, just for a couple of hours?"

"Who are Roger and Rebecca?" asked Ben.

"They're my boss's kids. He was looking after them today, but now he has a meeting he can't miss."

"I don't mind. Do you, Ben?" said Kate.

"Don't think so. What are the kids like?" Ben asked Kate's mom.

"I've never met them," she said, "but I'm sure you'll all like each other."

• • • • • • • • • • • • • 141 • • • • • • • • • • • • • *Remember Your Manners*

Two hours later, Roger and Rebecca were dropped off at Kate's house. Kate's mom introduced everyone and then said, "I'll leave you kids to play. Why don't you go into Kate's room?"

As soon as the four of them were on their own, Roger said to Ben, "Why are you friends with a girl?"

And, Rebecca said to Kate, "Why are you friends with a boy?"

"Because I like her," said Ben to Roger, puzzled.

"Because he's good fun," said Kate to Rebecca.

They all stood in silence for a moment. "Want to get some juice and cookies?" Ben asked Kate.

"Good idea," said Kate.

When the two of them were in the kitchen, Ben said, "This is going to be hard work!"

"I know!" said Kate. Then, they heard giggling from her room.

"Sounds like they've cheered up," said Ben. They loaded a tray with cookies and juice, and Kate carried it up the stairs.

When they got to the door, they heard Rebecca say, "They're coming. Put it back. Quick!"

"What's going on?" said Kate, coming into the room.

Roger and Rebecca were sitting on her bed. They had smiles on their faces, but somehow they weren't kind, friendly smiles.

Then, Kate noticed that her journal, which she kept on her desk, was now on the bed next to Roger and Rebecca.

"Have you been reading my journal?" Kate put the tray down.

"No," said Roger trying not to smile.

"It fell off the desk," said Rebecca.

"That's not true!" said Ben. "Don't you know journals are private?"

"She shouldn't have left it out on her desk," said Roger.

Kate stared at him for a moment. Then, she said, "I didn't think I had to hide it. Everyone I know respects my privacy."

"Calm down," said Roger. "It was boring anyway. You don't even say you love Ben! But, by the way, nice book!"

"Let's go into the living room and watch a movie," said Ben angrily. "At least we won't have to talk then."

Halfway through the movie, Kate's mom came into the room with some more juice. She walked in front of the TV on the way to the coffee table.

"Move!" said Ben, trying to see the screen.

"Excuse me!" said Kate's mom, surprised at Roger's rudeness. "You can come and get this in the kitchen when you're ready to be polite." She took the juice back out again.

"Who rattled her cage?" said Roger. "What does she expect if she stands in front of the TV!"

"Don't talk about my mom like that," said Kate. "You're in her house. Show some respect." They watched the rest of the movie in silence.

When the film was over, Roger went to get his sweater from Kate's room.

"Where's the bathroom?" asked Rebecca.

"Next to my room," Kate said.

"At least they will be gone soon," Kate whispered to Ben when they were alone.

Suddenly, they heard a shout. "Get out!" It was Roger.

Ben and Kate ran up the stairway towards her room. By the time they realized what had happened, it was too late to stop themselves from seeing what they saw.

Rebecca was standing at the open bathroom door, looking at an embarrassed, red-faced Roger, sitting on the toilet.

"I didn't know you were in there!" Rebecca shouted.

"You didn't knock!" yelled Roger

"You didn't lock the door!" she yelled back.

"I shouldn't have to! Don't you know bathrooms are private?"

Kate felt a bit sorry for Roger sitting on the toilet for everyone to see. She pulled the door shut.

"Now, you know how I felt when you read my journal, Roger," called Kate through the door. "And, by the way . . . "

"What?" shouted Roger.

"Nice underpants—I couldn't help but see them!"

The End

Unit 15
Learning Self-Control

Story Summary

Ethan and his cat, Zigzag, are both lively characters who have trouble controlling their behaviors. Ethan learns that when Zigzag is really upset and loses control, Ethan can calm the cat down by stroking the top of his head. When Ethan loses his temper with a friend and then shouts at his teacher, he and his mom need to have a serious talk about his own self-control.

Concepts

The story encourages children to consider that everyone has to deal with powerful feelings, such as anger and frustration, and must learn self-control. It will also help them think about strategies to regulate their own strong emotions.

Read the Story: "Crazy Cats"

Reproduce the story found on pages 151–157. Staple the pages together in numerical order and read them to the class.

Guided Questions

1. What were some of the crazy things Zigzag did as a kitten?

2. What were some of the crazy things Ethan did as a baby?

3. When Zigzag is angry, what calms him down?

4. What makes Ethan upset at school? What does he do that shows he has lost his temper?

5. Why, according to Ethan's mom, is it really important that people learn self-control?

6. In the story, Ethan can feel himself getting angrier and angrier, and then he shouts at his teacher. What feelings do you have when you are getting angry?

7. Ethan's mom tries to come up with ideas that might help Ethan's anger pass. What does she suggest?

8. What are some more ideas for how to control anger? (*counting to ten, taking deep breaths, stepping away to take a break*)

Role-Play Ideas

1. In groups of two or three, role-play a situation where someone loses her temper and does and says things she will wish she hadn't.

2. Act out the scene where Ethan sees the library book he wants, but this time Ethan acts politely and with self-control. How does the scene end differently?

3. Sometimes, people think it can be a cruel type of fun to see someone lose his temper. Role-play a scene where some children are trying to make another child mad, but he manages to keep his self-control.

What Is Self-Control?

1. Self-control means to always try your best.

2. Self-control means to be patient.

3. Self-control means to think before you talk.

4. Self-control means to think before you act.

Self-Control Means
Understandng How You Feel

This is me when I am
HAPPY.

This is me when I am
SAD.

This is me when I am
SCARED.

This is me when I am
ANGRY.

Control Your Temper

There are many things you can do to calm down
when you are angry. Try some of these ideas:

1. Admit that you feel angry.

2. Count to 10.

3. Go for a walk.

4. Use a calm voice when telling someone you are angry.

5. Relax and take some deep breaths.

6. Draw an idea of your own.

Crazy Cats

Zigzag had always been a crazy kind of cat. Even as a fluff ball of a kitten, he didn't play like other kittens. He didn't pat balls of wool or play around people's ankles. He would destroy the ball of wool and run all the way up people's legs. He swung from curtains, fell in the toilet bowl, terrified the dog, and got stuck in the washing machine.

Zigzag's mom, Muffet, would say, "You've got to be more careful. You want humans to think you're cute, not dangerous."

Muffet hoped her son would calm down when he got older. What Muffet didn't know was that her owner was just as worried about her son, Ethan. Ethan had always been a wild kind of boy. Even as a little baby, he didn't squeeze people's fingers like other babies; he bit them. He turned red and screamed when he didn't get his way. He threw things. He kicked people. As soon as he could speak, he used the worst words he knew and shouted them in the street. Ethan's mom hoped he would calm down when he got older.

When Ethan turned seven, his mom had decided that having a pet to look after might help him control his behavior. So, when Muffet had kittens, Ethan was allowed to choose one for his own. He named it Zigzag because of the wild way the kitten darted all over the place, always changing direction. Ethan liked to run around too. With Ethan and Zigzag, one was just as wild as the other.

One day, Zigzag was in a very bad mood. He scratched the dog; when the dog yelped, Zigzag spat in its face and hissed. When Ethan's mom tried to pull him away, Zigzag scratched her. Then, he hid behind the sofa.

Ethan went over and sat on the floor where he could reach Zigzag. He started to stroke the top of the kitten's head—it was the only part of Zigzag that Ethan could reach. Zigzag began to feel calmer and peaceful. He pushed his head up into Ethan's hand and he purred.

From then on, whenever Zigzag was out of control, Ethan gently stroked the top of his head, knowing it would calm him down. Each morning and evening, they sat on the sofa, and Ethan stroked Zigzag's head. Over the months, Zigzag grew calmer.

One day, Ethan got really upset at school. His friend, Michael, had taken the book Ethan wanted to read from the library.

"I wanted that—it's mine!" Ethan said and tried to pull the book right out of Michael's hand.

Michael held on. The book ripped.

"Idiot!" yelled Ethan. "That was your fault!"

"Ethan! I saw that!" The boys hadn't noticed their teacher coming over. "What on earth do you think you are doing?"

Ethan felt angry. He was sure that at any moment he would do something terrible. The feeling rose and rose in him, until he knew he was about to start shouting.

"It's none of your business!" he yelled at his teacher. "Leave me alone!"

Ethan's mom was called into the school. The principal said Ethan's lack of self-control was a problem. His mom promised they would take this seriously.

"It's a pity I can't stroke the top of your head, like you do to Zigzag," his mom said on the way home.

Ethan was still angry. He didn't answer her.

"We all get angry, Ethan. But, we all have to control our anger. Otherwise, the world would be crazy. Imagine if every cat behaved like Zigzag without you to stroke his head and calm him down."

"Everyone would live in fear of cats!" he said.

"Exactly." His mom suddenly looked serious. "I don't want your friends and family to live in fear of you. The reasons why people get angry are different, but everyone feels angry sometimes. What is important is that people find a way to control how they react to angry feelings." She reached over and patted his knee.

"You found a way to help Zigzag. Now, I want to find a way to help you."

"Having Zigzag with me would help," said Ethan.

"Why don't you think of Zigzag when you're going to lose your temper. Think about him doing the silliest thing and it might help your anger pass."

Ethan didn't say anything, but he thought he might try it.

His mom chuckled and said, "It reminded me of something."

"What?" asked Ethan.

"Your grandmother lost her temper with people. But, she was a kind woman and knew she had to find a way to control how she acted."

"What did she do?" asked Ethan.

"She'd take a good look at the people who were annoying her and then she'd imagine them standing in their underwear. It never failed."

The two of them laughed at the thought of Ethan's grandma picturing people in their underwear.

"I might try that," Ethan said, "but I'll try thinking of Zigzag acting silly first."

The End

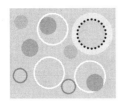

Correlations to the Standards

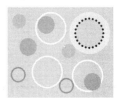

Correlation to Learning to *Read and Write: Developmentally Appropriate Practices for Young Children, Standards for the English Language Arts,* and *National Curriculum Standards for Social Studies*

This book supports the recommended teaching practices outlined in the NAEYC/IRA position statement *Learning to Read and Write: Developmentally Appropriate Practices for Young Children,* the NCTE/IRA *Standards for the English Language Arts,* and *selected examples in the National Curriculum Standards for Social Studies.*

NAEYC/IRA Position Statement
—— Learning to Read and Write: Developmentally Appropriate Practices for Young Children ——

The activities in this book support the following recommended teaching practices for Kindergarten and Primary students:

1. **Teachers read to children daily and provide opportunities for students to independently read both fiction and nonfiction texts.** Teachers read the reproducible story books in *Remember Your Manners* to students, while students read information on posters and worksheets from the book independently.

2. **Teachers provide opportunities for students to write many different kinds of texts for different purposes.** Students write words and sentences on selected teaching posters and worksheets in *Remember Your Manners.*

3. **Teachers provide challenging instruction that expands children's knowledge of their world and expands vocabulary.** *Remember Your Manners* presents vocabulary related to manners and good character to students.

———————————— NCTE/IRA Standards for the English Language Arts ————————————

Selected activities in this book support the following standards:

1. **Students read many different types of print and nonprint texts for a variety of purposes.** Teachers read reproducible storybooks to students, and students read the pictures and text on posters and worksheets while doing the activities in *Remember Your Manners.*

2. **Students use a variety of strategies to build meaning while reading.** Students participate in class discussions and role plays after reading or listening to the stories in *Remember Your Manners* in order to better comprehend the concepts in them.

3. **Students communicate in spoken, written, and visual form, for a variety of purposes and a variety of audiences.** Students speak, write, and draw while doing the activities in *Remember Your Manners.*

4. **Students become participating members of a variety of literacy communities.** The discussions and role plays in *Remember Your Manners* help teachers build a classroom literacy community.

Activities in this book support the following paraphrased examples.

1. **Culture**
   Knowledge:
   - **Students understand how culture helps people solve problems in daily life.** *Remember Your Manners* presents culturally accepted manners and shows students how they apply to daily life.

   - **Students understand how people learn about their culture from other members of that culture.** The stories in *Remember Your Manners* illustrate different ways that children learn about accepted manners.

4. **Individual Development and Identity**
   Knowledge:
   - **Students understand that studying individual growth teaches us who we are as we grow and change.** *Remember Your Manners* shows how individuals grow and change as they use proper manners.

   - **Students understand concepts including growth, change, learning, self, family, and groups.** The stories in *Remember Your Manners* incorporate all of these concepts.

   - **Students understand that growing up physically, emotionally, and intellectually will change their identity and how they interact with others.** *Remember Your Manners* aids in emotional growth that improves students' interactions with others.

   - **Students understand that the people and institutions around them affect their individual choices.** *Remember Your Manners* shows students how other people can teach them about proper manners.

5. **Individuals, Groups, and Institutions**
   Knowledge:
   - **Students understand that people belong to groups and organizations that influence their ideas and behaviors.** *Remember Your Manners* teaches students about appropriate behaviors that members of their community expect them to have.

   - **Students understand ideas such as community, culture, role, competition, cooperation, rules, and norms.** *Remember Your Manners* presents rules and norms of communities to students.

   - **Students understand how the rules and ideas of the groups they belong to affect their lives.** *Remember Your Manners* shows students how the rules and norms of their community affect their behavior.

   Processes:
   - **Students ask and answer questions about the influences that people, groups, and institutions have on them.** Each story in *Remember Your Manners* has accompanying discussion questions in which students discuss how the people and organizations around them have influence on them.

- **Students describe the interactions between people, groups, and organizations.** In each unit of *Remember Your Manners,* students discuss the interactions between the characters in the story.

- **Students describe conflicts that can arise between people, groups, and organizations.** In each unit of *Remember Your Manners,* students discuss conflicts that arise between characters of that unit's story.

6. **Power, Authority, and Governance**
   Knowledge:
   - **Students understand that rules and laws create order and protect individuals in a society.** Students discuss the role of rules and laws in a society in the "Good Citizenship" chapter of this book.

   Processes:
   - **Students ask and answer questions about power, authority, and government in various institutions.** Students discuss power, authority, and government in the "Good Citizenship" chapter of this book.

   - **Students study issues related to the rights and responsibilities of people and organizations in relation to society.** Students learn about people's rights and responsibilities as members of a community throughout *Remember Your Manners.*

   Products:
   - **Students describe and present solutions to school or community problems.** Students do this in the discussions and role plays throughout *Remember Your Manners.*

7. **Production, Distribution, and Consumption**
   Knowledge:
   - **Students understand what people and groups may gain or give up when making a decision.** Students learn about the costs and benefits of their actions throughout *Remember Your Manners.*

10. **Civic Ideals and Practices**
    Knowledge:
    - **Students understand how they can have an effect on their society.** Students learn how their behavior affects the world around them throughout *Remember Your Manners.*

    - **Students understand concepts including: dignity, fairness, freedom, common good, rule of law, civics, rights, and responsibilities.** *Remember Your Manners* presents many of these concepts to students.